Classic Baking

with

HERSHEY'S®

Printed in the USA

ISBN #0-934474-62-1

TABLE OF CONTENTS

FAVORITE RECIPES
FROM MY COOKBOOK

Recipe Name	Page Number

CAKES AND FROSTINGS
COCOA MAYONNAISE CAKE

1¾ cups all-purpose flour
1 cup sugar
⅓ cup HERSHEY'S Cocoa
1½ teaspoons baking powder
1½ teaspoons baking soda

⅛ teaspoon salt
1 cup mayonnaise
1 cup water
2 teaspoons vanilla extract

Heat oven to 350°F. Grease and flour 13x9x2-inch baking pan or 10-inch tube pan. In large mixer bowl, stir together flour, sugar, cocoa, baking powder, baking soda and salt. Add mayonnaise, water and vanilla; beat on medium speed of electric mixer 3 minutes. Pour batter into prepared pan. Bake 40 minutes for rectangular pan or 45 to 50 minutes for tube pan or until wooden pick inserted in center comes out clean. Cool 10 minutes; remove from pan. Cool completely; frost as desired. 12 to 15 servings.

APPLE-CHIP SNACKING CAKE

2 eggs
½ cup vegetable oil
¼ cup apple juice
1 teaspoon vanilla extract
1¾ cups all-purpose flour
1 cup granulated sugar
½ teaspoon baking soda
½ teaspoon ground cinnamon
½ teaspoon salt

1½ cups chopped peeled tart apples
¾ cup HERSHEY'S Semi-Sweet
    Chocolate Chips or HERSHEY'S
    MINI CHIPS Semi-Sweet
    Chocolate
½ cup chopped nuts
Powdered sugar or whipped topping
    and ground cinnamon (optional)

Heat oven to 350°F. Grease and flour 9-inch square baking pan. In large mixing bowl, beat eggs slightly; add oil, apple juice and vanilla. In bowl, stir together flour, granulated sugar, baking soda, cinnamon and salt; stir into batter until blended. Add apples, chocolate chips and nuts; stir until well blended. Pour batter into prepared pan. Bake 40 to 45 minutes or until cake begins to pull away from sides of pan. Cool completely on wire rack. Sprinkle powdered sugar over top or serve with dollop of whipped topping sprinkled with cinnamon, if desired. 9 servings.

PEANUT BUTTER CAKE

½ cup (1 stick) butter or margarine,
    softened
1 cup REESE'S Creamy or Crunchy
    Peanut Butter
⅔ cup granulated sugar
⅔ cup packed light brown sugar

2 eggs
2 teaspoons vanilla extract
2¼ cups all-purpose flour
1½ teaspoons baking soda
½ teaspoon salt
1½ cups milk

Heat oven to 350°F. Grease 13x9x2-inch baking pan. In large mixer bowl, beat butter, peanut butter, granulated sugar, brown sugar, eggs and vanilla until well blended. Stir together flour, baking soda and salt; add alternately with milk to butter mixture, blending well after each addition. Spread batter into prepared pan. Bake 35 to 40 minutes or until wooden pick inserted in center comes out clean. Cool in pan on wire rack. Frost as desired. 12 to 16 servings.

EASY PEANUT BUTTER-CHOCOLATE CHIP CAKE

1 package (18.5 oz.) yellow cake mix
  (with pudding in the mix)
4 eggs
¾ cup water
⅓ cup vegetable oil

⅓ cup REESE'S Creamy Peanut
  Butter
1½ cups HERSHEY'S Semi-Sweet
  Chocolate Chips, divided
¼ cup chopped, unsalted peanuts

Heat oven to 350°F. Grease and lightly flour 13x9x2-inch baking pan. Prepare cake batter according to package directions using eggs, water and oil; blend in peanut butter. Spoon half of batter into prepared pan. Sprinkle ¾ cup chocolate chips over batter. Gently spread remaining batter over top. Sprinkle remaining ¾ cup chips and peanuts over batter. Bake 45 minutes or until wooden pick inserted in center comes out clean. Cool in pan on wire rack. Frost as desired. 12 to 15 servings.

CHOCOLATE CAKE WITH CRUMB TOPPING

1½ cups all-purpose flour
1 cup sugar
¼ cup HERSHEY'S Cocoa
1 teaspoon baking soda
½ teaspoon salt
1 cup water

¼ cup plus 2 tablespoons vegetable oil
1 tablespoon white vinegar
1 teaspoon vanilla extract
CRUMB TOPPING (recipe follows)
Whipped topping or ice cream
  (optional)

Heat oven to 350°F. Grease and flour 9-inch square baking pan. In medium bowl, stir together flour, sugar, cocoa, baking soda and salt. Add water, oil, vinegar and vanilla; beat with spoon or wire whisk just until batter is smooth and ingredients are well blended. Pour batter into prepared pan. Sprinkle CRUMB TOPPING over batter. Bake 35 minutes or until wooden pick inserted in center comes out clean. Cool in pan on wire rack. Serve with whipped topping or ice cream, if desired. About 9 servings.

CRUMB TOPPING: In small bowl, stir together ½ cup graham cracker crumbs, ¼ cup chopped nuts and 2 tablespoons melted butter or margarine. Stir in ½ cup HERS-HEY'S Semi-Sweet Chocolate Chips.

CHOCOLATE SOUR CREAM CAKE

1¾ cups all-purpose flour
1¾ cups sugar
¾ cup HERSHEY'S Cocoa
1½ teaspoons baking soda
1 teaspoon salt

⅔ cup butter or margarine, softened
2 cups (16 oz.) dairy sour cream
2 eggs
1 teaspoon vanilla extract
FUDGE FROSTING (page 11)

Heat oven to 350°F. Grease and flour 13x9x2-inch baking pan. In large mixer bowl, mix together flour, sugar, cocoa, baking soda and salt on low speed of electric mixer. Add butter, sour cream, eggs and vanilla; beat on medium speed 3 minutes. Pour batter into prepared pan. Bake 40 to 45 minutes or until wooden pick inserted in center comes out clean. Cool in pan on wire rack. Frost with FUDGE FROSTING. 12 to 15 servings.

CHOCOLATE CHIP ORANGE POUND CAKE

½ cup (1 stick) butter, softened
4 ounces (½ of 8-oz. pkg.) cream
cheese, softened
¾ cup sugar
2 eggs
1 teaspoon vanilla extract

¼ teaspoon grated orange peel
1 cup all-purpose flour
1 teaspoon baking powder
1 cup HERSHEY'S MINI CHIPS
Semi-Sweet Chocolate
Powdered sugar

Heat oven to 325°F. Grease and flour 9x5x3-inch loaf pan. Cut butter and cream cheese into 1-inch slices; place in bowl of food processor. Add sugar; process until smooth, about 30 seconds. Add eggs, vanilla and orange peel; process until blended, about 10 seconds. Add flour and baking powder; process until blended, about 10 seconds. Stir in chocolate chips. Pour batter into prepared pan. Bake 45 to 50 minutes or until cake pulls away from sides of pan. Cool 10 minutes; remove from pan. Cool completely on wire rack. Sprinkle powdered sugar over cake. About 10 servings.

QUICK & EASY CHOCOLATE CAKE

4 bars (4 oz.) HERSHEY'S
Unsweetened Baking Chocolate,
broken into pieces
¼ cup (½ stick) butter or margarine
1⅔ cups boiling water
2⅓ cups all-purpose flour

2 cups sugar
½ cup dairy sour cream
2 eggs
2 teaspoons baking soda
1 teaspoon salt
1 teaspoon vanilla extract

Heat oven to 350°F. Grease and flour 13x9x2-inch baking pan. In large mixer bowl, combine chocolate, butter and water; with spoon, stir until chocolate is melted and mixture is smooth. Add flour, sugar, sour cream, eggs, baking soda, salt and vanilla; beat on low speed of electric mixer until smooth. Pour batter into prepared pan. Bake 35 to 40 minutes or until wooden pick inserted in center comes out clean. Cool completely in pan on wire rack. Frost as desired. 12 to 15 servings.

FROSTY TUNNELS OF FUDGE CAKE

1 package (about 18.25 oz.) white or
yellow cake mix
1 jar (about 18 oz.) HERSHEY'S
Chocolate Shoppe Topping
(Banana Split Fudge,
Butterscotch Caramel Fudge,
Chocolate Caramel Fudge,
Chocolate Almond Fudge, or
Double Chocolate Fudge) *

3½ cups (8 oz.) frozen non-dairy
whipped topping, thawed
Maraschino cherries, drained
(optional)

Prepare cake batter. Bake in 13x9x2-inch baking pan according to package directions. Remove from oven; do NOT remove cake from pan. With handle of wooden spoon, immediately pierce cake to bottom of pan, making rows about 1-inch apart, covering length and width of cake. Immediately spread or pour fudge topping evenly over entire surface, making sure entire top is covered and mixture has flowed into holes. Cool completely on wire rack; spread whipped topping evenly over top of cake. Cover; refrigerate several hours or overnight until well chilled. Cut into pieces; garnish each piece with maraschino cherry, if desired. Refrigerate leftovers. 12 to 15 servings.

* HOT FUDGE VARIATION: Bake and poke holes in cake as directed above. Place open jar HERSHEY'S Hot Fudge Chocolate Shoppe Topping in microwave oven; heat as directed on label. Carefully spread fudge topping on cake; proceed as directed above.

COCOA-COLA CAKE

2 cups sugar
2 cups all-purpose flour
1/2 cup (1 stick) butter or margarine
1/2 cup vegetable oil
1/3 cup HERSHEY'S Cocoa
1 cup regular cola (not diet)
1 1/2 cups miniature marshmallows

1/2 cup buttermilk or sour milk*
1 teaspoon baking soda
2 eggs, slightly beaten
1 teaspoon vanilla extract
CHOCOLATE NUT FROSTING (page 11)

Heat oven to 350°F. Grease 13x9x2-inch baking pan. In large mixer bowl, stir together sugar and flour; set aside. In medium saucepan, combine butter, oil, cocoa and cola; cook over medium heat, stirring constantly until mixture boils. Add chocolate mixture to sugar mixture; beat until smooth. Stir in marshmallows. Add buttermilk, baking soda, eggs and vanilla; blend well. Pour batter into prepared pan. Bake 40 to 45 minutes or until wooden pick inserted in center comes out clean. Meanwhile, prepare CHOCOLATE NUT FROSTING; spread over warm cake. Cool completely in pan on wire rack. 12 to 15 servings.

* To sour milk: Use 1 1/2 teaspoons white vinegar plus milk to equal 1/2 cup.

CHOCOLATE BAR FILLED CHOCOLATE CUPCAKES

CHOCOLATE BAR FILLING (recipe follows)
3 cups all-purpose flour
2 cups sugar
2/3 cup HERSHEY'S Cocoa
2 teaspoons baking soda
1 teaspoon salt

2 cups water
2/3 cup vegetable oil
2 tablespoons white vinegar
2 teaspoons vanilla extract
2 HERSHEY'S Milk Chocolate Bars (7 oz.), broken into pieces

Prepare FILLING; set aside. Heat oven to 350°F. Paper-line 30 muffin cups (2 1/2 inches in diameter). In large mixer bowl, stir together flour, sugar, cocoa, baking soda and salt. Add water, oil, vinegar and vanilla; beat on medium speed of electric mixer 2 minutes. Fill each muffin cup 2/3 full with batter. Spoon 1 level tablespoon FILLING into center of each cupcake. Bake 20 to 25 minutes or until wooden pick inserted in cake portion comes out clean. Remove from pan to wire rack. Cool completely. Top each cupcake with chocolate bar piece. About 2 1/2 dozen cupcakes.

CHOCOLATE BAR FILLING

1 package (8 oz.) cream cheese, softened
1/3 cup sugar
1 egg

1/8 teaspoon salt
1 HERSHEY'S Milk Chocolate Bar (7 oz.), cut into 1/4 inch pieces

In small mixer bowl, beat cream cheese, sugar, egg and salt until smooth and creamy. Stir in chocolate bar pieces.

4

COCOA APPLE CAKE

1 cup (2 sticks) butter or margarine
2 cups sugar
3 eggs
1 tablespoon vanilla extract
2½ cups all-purpose flour
¼ cup HERSHEY'S Cocoa
1 teaspoon baking soda
¾ teaspoon ground cinnamon
½ teaspoon ground allspice

½ cup water
2 cups shredded, peeled apple (2 medium)
1 cup chopped nuts
1 cup HERSHEY'S Semi-Sweet Chocolate Chips
CHOCOLATE GLAZE (recipe follows)
VANILLA GLAZE (recipe follows)

Heat oven to 325°F. Grease and flour 12-cup fluted tube pan. In large mixer bowl, beat butter and sugar until light and fluffy. Add eggs and vanilla; blend well. Stir together flour, cocoa, baking soda, cinnamon and allspice; add alternately with water to butter mixture, beating until blended. Fold in apple, nuts and chocolate chips; blend well. Pour into prepared pan. Bake 60 to 70 minutes or until wooden pick inserted comes out clean. Cool 15 minutes on wire rack; invert onto serving plate. Cool completely. Drizzle CHOCO-LATE GLAZE over cake; drizzle VANILLA GLAZE over top. 12 to 14 servings.

CHOCOLATE GLAZE

1 tablespoon butter or margarine
1 tablespoon HERSHEY'S Cocoa
1 tablespoon water

½ cup powdered sugar
¼ teaspoon vanilla extract

In small saucepan over low heat, melt butter; stir in cocoa and water. Cook, stirring constantly, until slightly thickened. Remove from heat. Gradually add powdered sugar and vanilla, beating with wire whisk until smooth.

VANILLA GLAZE: In small bowl, stir together ¼ cup powdered sugar and 1 to 2 teaspoons milk until smooth.

SPICY BUTTERSCOTCH SNACK CAKE

1 cup (2 sticks) butter or margarine, softened
1 cup sugar
2 eggs
½ teaspoon vanilla extract
½ cup applesauce
2½ cups all-purpose flour

1 teaspoon baking soda
1½ to 2 teaspoons ground cinnamon
½ teaspoon salt
1⅔ cups (10-oz. pkg.) HERSHEY'S Butterscotch Chips
1 cup chopped pecans (optional)
Powdered sugar (optional)

Heat oven to 350°F. Lightly grease 13x9x2-inch baking pan. In large mixer bowl, beat butter and sugar until well blended. Add eggs and vanilla; blend thoroughly. Mix in applesauce. In small bowl, stir together flour, baking soda, cinnamon and salt; gradually add to butter mixture, mixing well. Stir in butterscotch chips and pecans, if desired. Spread in prepared pan. Bake 35 to 40 minutes or until wooden pick inserted in center comes out clean. Cool completely in pan on wire rack. Sprinkle with powdered sugar, if desired. About 12 servings.

CHOCOLATE BUTTERMILK CAKE

1⅔ cups all-purpose flour
1½ cups sugar
⅔ cup HERSHEY'S Cocoa
1½ teaspoons baking soda
1 teaspoon salt
½ cup shortening

1½ cups buttermilk
1 teaspoon vanilla extract
2 eggs
HERSHEY'S CHOCOLATE
    FROSTING (page 11)

Heat oven to 350°F. Grease and flour 13x9x2-inch baking pan. In large mixer bowl, stir together all ingredients except JIFFY CHOCOLATE FROSTING. Blend on low speed of electric mixer 30 seconds, scraping bottom and sides of bowl constantly. Increase speed to medium; beat 3 minutes, scraping bowl occasionally. Pour batter into prepared pan. Bake 35 to 40 minutes or until wooden pick inserted in center comes out clean. Cool in pan on wire rack. Frost with HERSHEY'S CHOCOLATE FROSTING. 12 to 15 servings.

LICKETY-SPLIT COCOA CAKE

1½ cups all-purpose flour
1 cup sugar
¼ cup HERSHEY'S Cocoa
1 teaspoon baking soda
½ teaspoon salt
1 cup water

¼ cup plus 2 tablespoons vegetable oil
1 tablespoon white vinegar
1 teaspoon vanilla extract
LICKETY-SPLIT COCOA FROSTING
    (page 11)

Heat oven to 350°F. Grease and flour 8-inch square or 9-inch round baking pan. In large bowl, stir together flour, sugar, cocoa, baking soda and salt. Add water, oil, vinegar and vanilla; beat with spoon or wire whisk just until batter is smooth and ingredients are well blended. Pour batter into prepared pan. Bake 35 to 40 minutes or until wooden pick inserted in center comes out clean. Cool in pan; frost with LICKETY-SPLIT COCOA FROSTING. 8 to 10 servings.

DEEP DARK CHOCOLATE CAKE

2 cups sugar
1¾ cups all-purpose flour
¾ cup HERSHEY'S Cocoa or
    HERSHEY'S European Style
    Cocoa
1½ teaspoons baking powder
1½ teaspoons baking soda
1 teaspoon salt

2 eggs
1 cup milk
½ cup vegetable oil
2 teaspoons vanilla extract
1 cup boiling water
ONE-BOWL BUTTERCREAM
    FROSTING (page 11)

Heat oven to 350°F. Grease and flour two 9-inch round baking pans or one 13x9x2-inch baking pan. In large mixer bowl, stir together sugar, flour, cocoa, baking powder, baking soda and salt. Add eggs, milk, oil and vanilla; beat on medium speed of electric mixer 2 minutes. Remove from mixer; stir in boiling water (batter will be thin). Pour batter into prepared pans. Bake 30 to 35 minutes for round pans, 35 to 40 minutes for rectangular pan or until wooden pick inserted in center comes out clean. Cool 10 minutes; remove from pans to wire racks. Cool completely. (Cake may be left in rectangular pan, if desired.) Frost with ONE-BOWL BUTTERCREAM FROSTING. 8 to 10 servings.

HERSHEY BAR CAKE

1 HERSHEY'S Milk Chocolate Bar (7
   oz.), broken into pieces
¼ cup (½ stick) butter or margarine
1⅔ cups boiling water
2⅓ cups all-purpose flour
2 cups packed light brown sugar

2 teaspoons baking soda
1 teaspoon salt
2 eggs
½ cup dairy sour cream
1 teaspoon vanilla extract

Heat oven to 350°F. Grease and flour 13x9x2-inch baking pan. In bowl, combine chocolate bar pieces, butter and boiling water; stir until chocolate is melted and mixture is smooth. In large mixer bowl, stir together flour, brown sugar, baking soda and salt; gradually add chocolate mixture, beating until thoroughly blended. Blend in eggs, sour cream and vanilla; beat 1 minute on medium speed. Pour batter into prepared pan. Bake 35 to 40 minutes or until wooden pick inserted in center comes out clean. Cool completely in pan on wire rack; frost as desired. 12 to 15 servings.

CHOCOLATETOWN SPECIAL CAKE

½ cup HERSHEY'S Cocoa or
   HERSHEY'S European Style
   Cocoa
½ cup boiling water
⅔ cup shortening
1¾ cups sugar
1 teaspoon vanilla extract

2 eggs
2¼ cups all-purpose flour
1½ teaspoons baking soda
½ teaspoon salt
1⅓ cups buttermilk or sour milk*
ONE-BOWL BUTTERCREAM
   FROSTING (page 11)

Heat oven to 350°F. Grease and flour two 9-inch round baking pans. In small bowl, stir together cocoa and water until smooth; set aside. In large mixer bowl, beat shortening, sugar and vanilla until light and fluffy. Add eggs; beat well. Stir together flour, baking soda and salt; add to shortening mixture alternately with buttermilk. Blend in cocoa mixture; beat well. Pour batter into prepared pans. Bake 35 to 40 minutes or until wooden pick inserted in center comes out clean. Cool 10 minutes; remove from pans to wire racks. Cool completely. Frost with ONE-BOWL BUTTERCREAM FROSTING. 8 to 10 servings.

* To Sour Milk: Use 4 teaspoons white vinegar plus milk to equal 1⅓ cups.

GEORGIA PEANUT BUTTER CAKE

2 cups sugar
2 cups all-purpose flour
1 teaspoon baking powder
1 cup buttermilk or sour milk*
1 cup REESE'S Creamy Peanut Butter

½ cup (1 stick) butter or margarine,
   softened
½ cup vegetable oil
5 eggs
1 cup flaked coconut
1 teaspoon vanilla extract
GEORGIA PEANUT BUTTER
   FROSTING (page 12)

Heat oven to 350°F. Grease and flour three 9-inch round baking pans. In large mixer bowl, combine all ingredients. Beat on low speed of electric mixer until all ingredients are moistened. Beat on medium speed 2 to 3 minutes or until well blended. Pour batter into prepared pans. Bake 25 to 30 minutes or until wooden pick inserted in center comes out clean. Cool 10 minutes; remove from pans to wire racks. Cool completely. Frost with GEORGIA PEANUT BUTTER FROSTING. 10 to 12 servings.

OLD-FASHIONED CHOCOLATE CAKE

¾ cup (1½ sticks) butter or
  margarine, softened
1⅔ cups sugar
3 eggs
1 teaspoon vanilla extract
2 cups all-purpose flour
⅔ cup HERSHEY'S Cocoa
1¼ teaspoons baking soda

1 teaspoon salt
¼ teaspoon baking powder
1⅓ cups water
½ cup finely crushed hard peppermint
  candy (optional)
ONE-BOWL BUTTERCREAM
  FROSTING (page 11)

Heat oven to 350°F. Grease and flour two 9-inch round baking pans or one 13x9x2-inch baking pan. In large mixer bowl, combine butter, sugar, eggs and vanilla; beat on high speed of electric mixer 3 minutes. In separate bowl, stir together flour, cocoa, baking soda, salt and baking powder; add alternately with water to butter mixture. Blend just until combined; add candy, if desired. Pour batter into prepared pans. Bake 30 to 35 minutes or until wooden pick inserted in center comes out clean. Cool 10 minutes; remove from pans to wire racks. Cool completely; frost with ONE-BOWL BUTTERCREAM FROSTING. 8 to 10 servings.

FEATHERY FUDGE CAKE

2½ bars (2½ oz.) HERSHEY'S
  Unsweetened Baking Chocolate,
  broken into pieces
¾ cup (1½ sticks) butter or
  margarine, softened
2 cups sugar

1 teaspoon vanilla extract
2 eggs
2¼ cups all-purpose flour
1¼ teaspoons baking soda
½ teaspoon salt
1⅓ cups water

Heat oven to 350°F. In small microwave-safe bowl, place chocolate. Microwave at HIGH (100%) 1½ to 2 minutes or until smooth when stirred; set aside to cool slightly. Grease and flour two 9-inch round baking pans. In large mixer bowl, beat butter, sugar and vanilla until light and fluffy. Add eggs and cooled chocolate; blend well. Stir together flour, baking soda and salt; add alternately with water to butter mixture. Pour batter into prepared pans. Bake 35 to 40 minutes or until wooden pick inserted in center comes out clean. Cool 10 minutes; remove from pans to wire racks. Cool completely. Frost as desired. 10 to 12 servings.

BLACK MAGIC CAKE

2 cups sugar
1¾ cups all-purpose flour
¾ cup HERSHEY'S Cocoa
2 teaspoons baking soda
1 teaspoon baking powder
1 teaspoon salt
2 eggs

1 cup strong black coffee or 2
  teaspoons powdered instant coffee
  plus 1 cup boiling water
1 cup buttermilk or sour milk*
½ cup vegetable oil
1 teaspoon vanilla extract

Heat oven to 350°F. Grease and flour two 9-inch round baking pans or one 13x9x2-inch baking pan. In large mixer bowl, stir together sugar, flour, cocoa, baking soda, baking powder and salt. Add eggs, coffee, buttermilk, oil and vanilla; beat on medium speed of electric mixer 2 minutes (batter will be thin). Pour batter into prepared pan. Bake 30 to 35 minutes for round pans, 35 to 40 minutes for rectangular pan or until wooden pick inserted in center comes out clean. Cool 10 minutes; remove from pans to wire racks. Cool completely. Frost as desired. 10 to 12 servings.

* To sour milk: Use 1 tablespoon white vinegar plus milk to equal 1 cup.

CHOCOLATE BAR CAKE

1 HERSHEY'S Milk Chocolate Bar (7 oz.), broken into pieces
½ cup (1 stick) butter or margarine, softened
1 cup boiling water
2 cups all-purpose flour
1½ cups sugar
½ cup HERSHEY'S Cocoa
2 teaspoons baking soda
1 teaspoon salt
2 eggs
½ cup dairy sour cream
1 teaspoon vanilla extract
VANILLA GLAZE (recipe follows)

Heat oven to 350°F. Grease and flour 12-cup fluted tube pan. In small bowl, stir together chocolate bar pieces, butter and water until chocolate is melted. In large mixer bowl, stir together flour, sugar, cocoa, baking soda and salt; gradually add chocolate mixture, beating until thoroughly blended. Add eggs, sour cream and vanilla; blend well. Beat on medium speed of electric mixer 1 minute. Pour batter into prepared pan. Bake 50 to 55 minutes or until wooden pick inserted in center comes out clean. Cool 10 minutes; remove from pan to wire rack. Cool completely. Drizzle VANILLA GLAZE over cake. 10 to 12 servings.

VANILLA GLAZE: In medium microwave-safe bowl, place ¼ cup (½ stick) butter or margarine. Microwave at HIGH (100%) 30 seconds or until melted. Gradually stir in 2 cups powdered sugar, 2 to 3 tablespoons hot water and 1 teaspoon vanilla extract; beat with wire whisk until smooth and slightly thickened. About 1¼ cups glaze.

CLASSIC HERSHEY BAR CAKE

1 cup (2 sticks) butter or margarine, softened
1¼ cups granulated sugar
4 eggs
6 HERSHEY'S Milk Chocolate Bars (1.55 oz. each), melted
2½ cups all-purpose flour
¼ teaspoon baking soda
Dash salt
1 cup buttermilk or sour milk*
½ cup (5½ oz. can) HERSHEY'S Syrup
2 teaspoons vanilla extract
1 cup chopped pecans
Powdered sugar (optional)

Heat oven to 350°F. Grease and flour 10-inch tube pan or 12-cup fluted tube pan. In large mixer bowl, beat butter until creamy; gradually add granulated sugar, beating on medium speed of electric mixer until well blended. Add eggs, one at a time, beating well after each addition. Add chocolate; beat until blended. Stir together flour, baking soda and salt; add to chocolate mixture alternately with buttermilk, beating until blended. Add syrup and vanilla; beat until blended. Stir in pecans. Pour batter into prepared pan. Bake 1 hour and 15 minutes or until wooden pick inserted in center of cake comes out clean. Cool 10 minutes; remove from pan to wire rack. Cool completely. Sift powdered sugar over top, if desired. 12 to 16 servings.

* To sour milk: Use 1 tablespoon white vinegar plus milk to equal 1 cup.

CHOCOLATETOWN CHOCOLATE CHIP CAKE

3 cups all-purpose flour
2 teaspoons baking powder
1/2 teaspoon salt
1 cup (2 sticks) butter or margarine,
  softened
1 cup granulated sugar
1 cup packed light brown sugar

1 1/2 teaspoons vanilla extract
3 eggs
1 cup milk
1 1/2 cups HERSHEY'S MINI CHIPS
  Semi-Sweet Chocolate
SATINY MINI CHIPS GLAZE (recipe
  follows)

Heat oven to 350°F. Grease and flour 12-cup fluted tube pan or 13x9x2-inch baking pan. In medium bowl, stir together flour, baking powder and salt. In large mixer bowl, beat butter, granulated sugar, brown sugar and vanilla until light and fluffy. Add eggs, one at a time, beating well after each addition. Add flour mixture alternately with milk to butter mixture, beating well after each addition. Stir in small chocolate chips. Pour BATTER into prepared pan. Bake 55 to 60 minutes for fluted tube pan and 45 to 50 minutes for rectangular pan or until wooden pick inserted in center comes out clean. Cool 15 minutes; remove from pan to wire rack. Cool completely. Glaze with SATINY MINI CHIPS GLAZE. 10 to 12 servings.

SATINY MINI CHIPS GLAZE: In small saucepan, combine 2 tablespoons sugar and 2 tablespoons water. Heat to boiling; stir until sugar is dissolved. Remove from heat. Immediately add 1/2 cup HERSHEY'S MINI CHIPS Semi-Sweet Chocolate, stirring until melted. Remove from heat. Stir until desired consistency. About 1/2 cup glaze.

RHAPSODY CHOCOLATE CAKE

1 SYMPHONY Milk Chocolate Bar or
  Milk Chocolate Bar With
  Almonds & Toffee Chips (7 oz.),
  broken into pieces*
1/2 cup (1 stick) butter or margarine,
  softened
1 cup boiling water
2 cups all-purpose flour

1 1/2 cups sugar
1/2 cup HERSHEY'S Cocoa
2 teaspoons baking soda
1 teaspoon salt
2 eggs
1/2 cup dairy sour cream
1 teaspoon vanilla extract
VANILLA GLAZE (recipe follows)

Heat oven to 350°F. Grease and flour 12-cup fluted tube pan. In small bowl, stir together chocolate bar pieces, butter and water until chocolate is melted. In large mixer bowl, stir together flour, sugar, cocoa, baking soda and salt; gradually add chocolate mixture, beating until thoroughly blended. Add eggs, sour cream and vanilla; blend well. Beat on medium speed of electric mixer 1 minute. Pour batter into prepared pan. Bake 55 to 60 minutes or until wooden pick inserted in center comes out clean. Cool 10 minutes; remove from pan to wire rack. Cool completely. Drizzle VANILLA GLAZE over cake. 10 to 12 servings.

VANILLA GLAZE: In medium microwave-safe bowl, place 1/4 cup (1/2 stick) butter or margarine. Microwave at HIGH (100%) 30 seconds or until melted. Gradually stir in 2 cups powdered sugar, 2 to 3 tablespoons hot water and 1 teaspoon vanilla extract; beat with wire whisk until smooth and slightly thickened. About 1 1/4 cups glaze.

* 5 SYMPHONY Milk Chocolate Bars or Milk Chocolate Bars With Almonds & Toffee Chips (1.4 oz. each) may be substituted.

FUDGE FROSTING

3 tablespoons butter or margarine
1/3 cup HERSHEY'S Cocoa
1 1/3 cups powdered sugar

2 to 3 tablespoons milk
1/2 teaspoon vanilla extract

In small saucepan over low heat, melt butter. Add cocoa; cook, stirring constantly, just until mixture begins to boil. Pour mixture into small mixer bowl; cool completely. To cocoa mixture, add powdered sugar alternately with milk, beating to spreading consistency. Blend in vanilla. About 1 cup frosting.

CHOCOLATE NUT FROSTING

3 2/3 cups (1 lb.) powdered sugar
1/2 cup (1 stick) butter or margarine
6 tablespoons regular cola (not diet)

3 tablespoons HERSHEY'S Cocoa
1/2 to 1 cup coarsely chopped pecans
1 teaspoon vanilla extract

In small mixer bowl, place powdered sugar; set aside. In small saucepan over medium heat, combine butter, cola and cocoa; cook, stirring constantly, until mixture boils. Pour hot mixture over powdered sugar; beat until smooth and slightly thickened. Stir in pecans and vanilla. About 2 1/2 cups frosting.

HERSHEY'S CHOCOLATE FROSTING

1 cup HERSHEY'S Semi-Sweet
   Chocolate Chips

1 cup powdered sugar
1/3 cup evaporated milk

In small microwave-safe bowl, place chocolate chips. Microwave at HIGH (100%) 1 minute; stir. Microwave at HIGH additional 30 seconds or until melted and smooth when stirred. Gradually add powdered sugar and evaporated milk, beating until smooth. About 1 1/4 cups frosting.

LICKETY-SPLIT COCOA FROSTING

3 tablespoons butter or margarine,
   softened
1/4 cup HERSHEY'S Cocoa

1 1/4 cups powdered sugar
2 to 3 tablespoons milk
1/2 teaspoon vanilla extract

In small mixer bowl, beat butter until light and fluffy. Add cocoa, powdered sugar, milk and vanilla; beat until smooth and of desired consistency. About 1 cup frosting.

ONE-BOWL BUTTERCREAM FROSTING

6 tablespoons butter or margarine,
   softened
2 2/3 cups powdered sugar
1/2 cup HERSHEY'S Cocoa or
   HERSHEY'S European Style
   Cocoa

1/3 cup milk
1 teaspoon vanilla extract

In small mixer bowl, beat butter. Add powdered sugar and cocoa alternately with milk; beat to spreading consistency (additional milk may be needed). Blend in vanilla. About 2 cups frosting.

GEORGIA PEANUT BUTTER FROSTING

1 package (8 oz.) cream cheese,
   softened
1/2 cup (1 stick) butter or margarine,
   softened

1/2 cup REESE'S Creamy Peanut
   Butter
3 2/3 cups (1-lb.box) powdered sugar
1 teaspoon vanilla extract

In large mixer bowl, beat cream cheese, butter and peanut butter until creamy. Gradually add powdered sugar and vanilla, beating until well blended. About 3 3/4 cups frosting.

    * To sour milk: Use 1 tablespoon white vinegar plus milk to equal 1 cup.

PEANUT BUTTER FROSTING

1/4 cup water
1/2 cup REESE'S Creamy Peanut
   Butter

1 teaspoon vanilla extract
1 1/2 to 2 cups powdered sugar

In small mixer bowl, gradually beat water into peanut butter, beating until smooth. Blend in vanilla. Add powdered sugar; beat to spreading consistency. About 1 1/2 cups frosting.

FLUFFY REESE'S PEANUT BUTTER FROSTING

1 cup milk
3 tablespoons all-purpose flour
1/2 cup REESE'S Creamy Peanut
   Butter

1/2 cup shortening
1 cup sugar
1 teaspoon vanilla extract
Dash salt

In small saucepan, gradually stir milk into flour. Cook over low heat, stirring constantly, until very thick. Transfer to small mixer bowl; press plastic wrap directly on surface. Cool to room temperature, about 1/2 hour. Add peanut butter, shortening, sugar, vanilla and salt. Beat on high speed of electric mixer until mixture becomes fluffy and sugar is completely dissolved. About 3 cups frosting.

QUICK & EASY CHOCOLATE FROSTING

3 bars (3 oz.) HERSHEY'S
   Unsweetened Baking Chocolate,
   broken into pieces
1 cup miniature marshmallows

1/2 cup (1 stick) butter or margarine,
   softened
1/3 cup milk
2 1/2 cups powdered sugar
1/2 teaspoon vanilla extract

In medium saucepan over low heat, melt chocolate, stirring constantly. Add marshmallows; stir frequently until melted. (Mixture will be very thick and will pull away from sides of pan.) Spoon mixture into small mixer bowl; beat in butter and milk until smooth. Add sugar and vanilla; beat to desired consistency. About 2 1/4 cups frosting.

CHOCOLATE BUTTERCREAM FROSTING

3 tablespoons butter or margarine,
   softened
1/3 cup HERSHEY'S Cocoa

1 cup powdered sugar
3 tablespoons milk
1/2 teaspoon vanilla extract

In small mixer bowl, beat butter. Add cocoa and powdered sugar alternately with milk. Beat to spreading consistency. Blend in vanilla. About 1 cup frosting.

CHEESECAKES, TORTES, COFFEECAKES, BREADS
CHOCOLATE DRIZZLED PEANUT BUTTER CHEESECAKE

3 packages (8 oz. each) cream
   cheese, softened
¾ cup sugar
1⅔ cups (10-oz. pkg.) REESE'S
   Peanut Butter Chips
¼ cup milk

4 eggs
1 teaspoon vanilla extract
GRAHAM CRACKER CRUST (recipe
   follows)
CHOCOLATE DRIZZLE (recipe
   follows)

Heat oven to 450°F. In large mixer bowl, beat cream cheese and sugar on medium speed of electric mixer until smooth. In small microwave-safe bowl, place peanut butter chips and milk. Microwave at HIGH (100%) 1 minute; stir. If necessary, microwave at HIGH an additional 15 seconds at a time, stirring after each heating, just until chips are melted when stirred. Blend peanut butter chip mixture into cream cheese mixture. Add eggs, one at a time, mixing well after each addition. Stir in vanilla. Pour mixture over prepared GRAHAM CRACKER CRUST. Bake 10 minutes. Reduce oven temperature to 250°F.; continue baking 40 minutes. Remove from oven to wire rack. With knife, loosen cake from side of pan. Cool completely; remove side of pan. Prepare CHOCOLATE DRIZ-ZLE; drizzle over cheesecake. Refrigerate before serving. Cover; refrigerate leftovers. 12 servings.

GRAHAM CRACKER CRUST: Heat oven to 325°F. In small bowl, stir together 1 cup graham cracker crumbs, 3 tablespoons sugar and 3 tablespoons melted butter or margarine. Press mixture onto bottom of 9-inch springform pan. Bake 10 minutes. Remove from oven.

CHOCOLATE DRIZZLE: In small microwave-safe bowl, place ½ cup HERS-HEY'S Semi-Sweet Chocolate Chips and 1 tablespoon shortening. Microwave at HIGH (100%) 30 seconds; stir. If necessary, microwave at HIGH an additional 20 seconds or until chocolate is melted and mixture is smooth when stirred.

SPECIAL DARK CHEESECAKE SQUARES

1 large orange
½ cup (1 stick) butter or margarine,
   softened
¼ cup plus ⅔ cup sugar, divided
¼ teaspoon salt
1¼ cups all-purpose flour

1 HERSHEY'S SPECIAL DARK
   Chocolate Bar (7 oz.), broken into
   pieces
2 packages (8 oz. each) cream
   cheese, softened
2 eggs

Line 8- or 9-inch square baking pan with foil, extending edges over sides of pan. Grate ½ teaspoon orange peel from orange and squeeze about 3 tablespoons juice; set aside. In small mixer bowl, beat butter, ¼ cup sugar, ¼ teaspoon orange peel and salt until smooth. At low speed of electric mixer, beat in flour until crumbly. Add enough orange juice (about 1 tablespoon) until dough holds together. Press dough onto bottom of prepared pan. Refrigerate 15 minutes. Heat oven to 350°F. Bake crust 20 to 25 minutes or until golden. Meanwhile, place chocolate pieces in medium microwave-safe bowl. Microwave at HIGH (100%) 1 minute or until chocolate is melted and smooth when stirred. In small mixer bowl, beat cream cheese with remaining ⅔ cup sugar until smooth. Add eggs, remaining ¼ teaspoon orange peel, remaining 2 tablespoons orange juice and melted chocolate; blend until smooth. Pour over crust. Bake 35 to 40 minutes or until cheesecake is firm and top is slightly puffed. Cool completely in pan on wire rack; refrigerate before serving. To serve, lift from pan using foil edges; cut into squares. Cover; refrigerate leftovers. About 20 servings.

CHOCOLATE CHIP CHEESECAKE

1½ cups graham cracker crumbs
⅓ cup HERSHEY'S Cocoa
⅓ cup sugar
⅓ cup butter or margarine, melted
3 packages (8 oz. each) cream
    cheese, softened

1 can (14 oz.) sweetened condensed
    milk
3 eggs
2 teaspoons vanilla extract
1 cup HERSHEY'S MINI CHIPS
    Semi-Sweet Chocolate, divided
1 teaspoon all-purpose flour

Heat oven to 300°F. In medium bowl, stir together graham cracker crumbs, cocoa, sugar and butter; press mixture onto bottom of 9-inch springform pan. In large mixer bowl, beat cream cheese until fluffy. Gradually add sweetened condensed milk, beating until smooth. Add eggs and vanilla; mix well. In small bowl, toss ½ cup small chocolate chips with flour to coat; stir into cheese mixture. Pour over prepared crust. Sprinkle remaining ½ cup chips evenly over top. Bake 1 hour. Turn off oven; allow to cool in oven 1 hour. Remove from oven. With knife, loosen cake from side of pan. Cool completely; remove side of pan. Refrigerate before serving. Cover; refrigerate leftovers. 10 to 12 servings.

TIP: For best distribution of chips throughout cheesecake, do not oversoften or overbeat cream cheese.

PAISLEY PRINT CHEESECAKE

3 packages (8 oz. each) cream
    cheese, softened
1 cup sugar, divided
½ cup dairy sour cream
2½ teaspoons vanilla extract, divided

3 tablespoons all-purpose flour
3 eggs
1½ bars (1½ oz.) HERSHEY'S
    Unsweetened Baking Chocolate,
    broken into pieces
GRAHAM CRUST (recipe follows)

Heat oven to 450°F. In large mixer bowl, combine cream cheese, ¾ cup sugar, sour cream and 2 teaspoons vanilla; beat on medium speed of electric mixer until smooth. Add flour, 1 tablespoon at a time, blending well. Add eggs; beat well. In small microwave-safe bowl, place chocolate. Microwave at HIGH (100%) 1 to 1½ minutes or just until chocolate is melted and smooth when stirred. Add 1½ cups cream cheese mixture, remaining ¼ cup sugar and remaining ½ teaspoon vanilla; blend well. Spoon plain and chocolate mixtures alternately into prepared GRAHAM CRUST, ending with dollops of chocolate on top; gently swirl with knife or spatula for paisley effect. Bake 10 minutes; reduce temperature to 250°F. Continue baking 35 minutes. Remove pan from oven to wire rack. With knife, loosen cake from side of pan. Cool completely; remove side of pan. Refrigerate before serving. Cover; refrigerate leftovers. 10 to 12 servings.

GRAHAM CRUST: Heat oven to 350°F. In small bowl, stir together 1 cup graham cracker crumbs and 2 tablespoons sugar; blend in ¼ cup melted butter or margarine, mixing well. Press mixture onto bottom and ½ inch up side of 9-inch springform pan. Bake 8 to 10 minutes. Cool.

GRAND FINALE CHEESECAKE

1 SYMPHONY Milk Chocolate Bar or
  Milk Chocolate Bar With
  Almonds & Toffee Chips (7 oz.),
  broken into pieces
4 packages (3 oz. each) cream
  cheese, softened
1/2 cup sugar

2 tablespoons HERSHEY'S Cocoa
1/8 teaspoon salt
2 eggs
1 teaspoon vanilla extract
ALMOND CRUST (recipe follows)
Whipped cream (optional)

Heat oven to 325°F. In small microwave-safe bowl, place chocolate. Microwave at HIGH (100%) 1 minute or until chocolate is melted and smooth when stirred. In large mixer bowl, beat cream cheese until fluffy. Stir together sugar, cocoa and salt; blend into cream cheese mixture. Add eggs and vanilla; blend well. Add melted chocolate; beat just until blended. Pour into prepared ALMOND CRUST. Bake 35 to 40 minutes or until almost set. Remove from oven to wire rack. With knife, loosen cake from side of pan. Cool completely; remove side of pan. Refrigerate. Just before serving, garnish with whipped cream, if desired. Cover; refrigerate leftovers. 8 servings.

ALMOND CRUST: In medium bowl, stir together 3/4 cup graham cracker crumbs, 2/3 cup chopped slivered almonds and 2 tablespoons sugar. Stir in 1/4 cup (1/2 stick) melted butter or margarine; blend well. Press mixture onto bottom and up side of 8-inch springform pan or round pan with removable bottom.

HERSHEY BAR CHEESECAKE

1 HERSHEY'S Milk Chocolate Bar (7
  oz.), broken into pieces
4 packages (3 oz. each) cream
  cheese, softened
3/4 cup sugar
2 tablespoons HERSHEY'S Cocoa

Dash salt
2 eggs
1/2 teaspoon vanilla extract
ALMOND CRUST (recipe follows)
SOUR CREAM TOPPING (optional,
  recipe follows)

Heat oven to 325°F. In small microwave-safe bowl, place chocolate. Microwave at HIGH (100%) 1 minute or until chocolate is melted and smooth when stirred. In large mixer bowl, beat cream cheese until light and fluffy. Stir together sugar, cocoa and salt; blend into cream cheese mixture. Add eggs and vanilla, blend well. Add melted chocolate; beat just until blended (do not overbeat). Pour batter into prepared ALMOND CRUST. Bake 35 to 40 minutes or until set. Remove from oven to wire rack. With knife, loosen cake from side of pan. Cool to room temperature; remove side of pan. Spread SOUR CREAM TOPPING over cheesecake, if desired. Refrigerate several hours before serving. Cover; refrigerate leftovers. 8 servings.

ALMOND CRUST: In medium bowl, stir together 3/4 cup graham cracker crumbs, 2/3 cup chopped slivered almonds and 2 tablespoons sugar. Stir in 1/4 cup (1/2 stick) melted butter or margarine; blend well. Press mixture onto bottom and up side of 8-inch springform pan or round pan with removable bottom.

SOUR CREAM TOPPING: In small bowl, stir together 1/2 cup dairy sour cream, 2 tablespoons sugar and 1/2 teaspoon vanilla extract.

VANILLA CITRUS CHEESECAKE WITH CHOCOLATE DRIZZLE

2 cups graham cracker crumbs
⅓ cup butter or margarine, melted
2 tablespoons plus 1½ cups sugar, divided
3 packages (8 oz. each) cream cheese, softened
4 eggs

1 teaspoon vanilla extract
1 teaspoon freshly grated orange peel
1⅔ cups (10-oz. pkg.) HERSHEY'S Vanilla Milk Chips
CHOCOLATE DRIZZLE (recipe follows)

Heat oven to 350°F. In small bowl, stir together crumbs, butter and 2 tablespoons sugar. Press mixture evenly onto bottom of 9-inch springform pan. Bake 5 minutes or just until golden brown; remove from oven (do not turn off oven). In large mixer bowl, beat cream cheese and remaining 1½ cups sugar until smooth. Add eggs, vanilla extract and orange peel; beat well. In small microwave-safe bowl, place vanilla milk chips. Microwave at HIGH (100%) 1 to 1½ minutes or until chips are melted and smooth when stirred vigorously. Blend into cream cheese mixture. Pour over crust. Bake 35 to 40 minutes or just until almost set. Remove from oven to wire rack. With knife, loosen cake from side of pan. Cool completely; remove side of pan. Refrigerate until firm before serving. Using tip of spoon, drizzle CHOCOLATE DRIZZLE across top of cheesecake. 10 to 12 servings.

CHOCOLATE DRIZZLE: In small microwave-safe bowl, place ½ cup HERSHEY'S Semi-Sweet Chocolate Chips and 1 tablespoon shortening. Microwave at HIGH (100%) 30 to 45 seconds or until chocolate is melted and mixture is smooth when stirred.

FUDGE TRUFFLE CHEESECAKE

2 cups (12-oz. pkg.) HERSHEY'S Semi-Sweet Chocolate Chips
3 packages (8 oz. each) cream cheese, softened
1 can (14 oz.) sweetened condensed milk

4 eggs
2 teaspoons vanilla extract
CHOCOLATE CRUMB CRUST (recipe follows)

Heat oven to 300°F. In microwave-safe bowl, place chocolate chips. Microwave at HIGH (100%) 1½ to 2 minutes or until chocolate is melted and smooth when stirred. In large mixer bowl, beat cream cheese until fluffy. Gradually beat in sweetened condensed milk until smooth. Add melted chocolate and remaining ingredients; mix well. Pour into prepared CHOCOLATE CRUMB CRUST. Bake 1 hour and 5 minutes or until center is set. Remove from oven to wire rack. With knife, loosen cake from side of pan. Cool completely; remove side of pan. Refrigerate before serving. Cover; refrigerate leftovers. 10 to 12 servings.

CHOCOLATE CRUMB CRUST: In medium bowl, stir together 1½ cups vanilla wafer crumbs, ½ cup powdered sugar, ⅓ cup HERSHEY'S Cocoa and ⅓ cup melted butter or margarine. Press firmly on bottom of 9-inch springform pan.

GERMAN CHOCOLATE CHEESECAKE

4 bars (4 oz.) HERSHEY'S Semi-
   Sweet Baking Chocolate, broken
   into pieces
3 packages (8 oz. each) cream
   cheese, softened
¾ cup sugar
½ cup dairy sour cream

2 teaspoons vanilla extract
2 tablespoons all-purpose flour
3 eggs
COCONUT-PECAN GRAHAM
   CRUST (recipe follows)
COCONUT-PECAN TOPPING (recipe
   follows)

Heat oven to 450°F. In small microwave-safe bowl, place chocolate. Microwave at HIGH (100%) 1 to 1½ minutes or until chocolate is melted and smooth when stirred. In large mixer bowl, combine cream cheese, sugar, sour cream and vanilla; beat on medium speed of electric mixer until smooth. Add flour, 1 tablespoon at a time, blending well. Add eggs and melted chocolate; blend well. Pour into prepared COCONUT-PECAN GRAHAM CRUST. Bake 10 minutes; without opening oven door, reduce oven temperature to 250°F. Continue baking 35 minutes; remove from oven. With knife, loosen cake from side of pan. Cool completely; remove side of pan. Prepare COCONUT-PECAN TOPPING. Spread topping over top of cake. Refrigerate until firm before serving. Cover; refrigerate leftovers. 10 to 12 servings.

COCONUT-PECAN GRAHAM CRUST

1 cup graham cracker crumbs
2 tablespoons sugar
⅓ cup butter or margarine, melted

¼ cup flaked coconut
¼ cup chopped pecans

Heat oven to 350°F. In small bowl, combine graham cracker crumbs and sugar. Stir in butter, coconut and pecans; mix thoroughly. Press mixture onto bottom and ½-inch up side of 9-inch springform pan. Bake 8 to 10 minutes. Cool.

COCONUT-PECAN TOPPING

½ cup (1 stick) butter or margarine
¼ cup packed light brown sugar
2 tablespoons light cream
2 tablespoons light corn syrup

1 cup flaked coconut
½ cup chopped pecans
1 teaspoon vanilla extract

In small saucepan, melt butter; add brown sugar, light cream and corn syrup. Cook over medium heat, stirring constantly, until smooth and bubbly. Remove from heat. Stir in coconut, pecans and vanilla. Cool slightly.

MICROWAVE DIRECTIONS: In microwave-safe bowl, place butter. Microwave at HIGH (100%) 30 seconds to 1 minute or until melted. Add brown sugar, light cream and corn syrup. Microwave at HIGH 2½ to 3 minutes, stirring every 30 seconds, until smooth and bubbly. Stir in remaining ingredients. Cool slightly.

BUTTERSCOTCH CHEESECAKE WITH CHOCOLATE DRIZZLE

GRAHAM CRACKER CRUST (recipe
follows)
3 packages (8 oz. each) cream
cheese, softened
1/2 cup sugar
2 tablespoons all-purpose flour

1 2/3 cups (10-oz. pkg.) HERSHEY'S
Butterscotch Chips
2 tablespoons milk
4 eggs
CHOCOLATE DRIZZLE (recipe
follows)

Prepare GRAHAM CRACKER CRUST. Heat oven to 350°F. In large mixer bowl, combine cream cheese, sugar and flour; beat on medium speed of electric mixer until smooth. In small microwave-safe bowl, place butterscotch chips and milk. Microwave at HIGH (100%) 1 minute; stir. If necessary, microwave at HIGH an additional 15 seconds at a time, stirring after each heating, just until chips are melted when stirred. Blend butterscotch mixture into cream cheese mixture. Add eggs, one at a time, mixing well after each addition. Pour mixture over crust. Bake 40 to 45 minutes or until center is almost set. Remove from oven to wire rack; loosen cake from side of pan. Cool completely; remove side of pan. Prepare CHOCOLATE DRIZZLE; drizzle over cheesecake. Store in refrigerator. 12 servings.

GRAHAM CRACKER CRUST: Heat oven to 325°F. In small bowl, stir together 1 cup graham cracker crumbs, 3 tablespoons sugar and 3 tablespoons melted butter or margarine. Press mixture onto bottom of 9-inch springform pan. Bake 10 minutes. Remove from oven.

CHOCOLATE DRIZZLE: In small microwave-safe bowl, place 1/2 cup HERSHEY'S Semi-Sweet Chocolate Chips and 1 tablespoon shortening. Microwave at HIGH (100%) 30 seconds; stir. If necessary, microwave at HIGH an additional 20 seconds or until chocolate is melted and mixture is smooth when stirred.

APPLE MINI CHIP TORTE

COOKIE DOUGH CRUST (recipe
follows)
4 packages (3 oz. each) cream
cheese, softened
1/3 cup sugar

1 egg
1/2 teaspoon vanilla extract
1 cup HERSHEY'S MINI CHIPS
Semi-Sweet Chocolate
APPLE TOPPING (recipe follows)

Heat oven to 400°F. Prepare COOKIE DOUGH CRUST; set aside. In large mixer bowl, beat cream cheese, sugar, egg and vanilla until smooth; stir in small chocolate chips. Pour cheese mixture into prepared CRUST; arrange apple topping over cheese filling. Bake 10 minutes; reduce oven temperature to 350°F. Continue baking 25 to 30 minutes or until crust is golden brown. Cool completely in pan on wire rack. 10 servings.

COOKIE DOUGH CRUST

1/3 cup butter or margarine
1/3 cup sugar
1 egg

1/4 teaspoon vanilla extract
1 1/2 cups all-purpose flour
1/2 teaspoon baking powder

In small mixer bowl, beat butter, sugar, egg and vanilla until creamy. Blend in flour and baking powder. With lightly floured fingers, evenly press dough on bottom and up sides of 9-inch round baking pan.

APPLE TOPPING: In bowl, toss 2 cups peeled, thinly sliced apples with 3 tablespoons sugar and 1/4 teaspoon ground cinnamon until apples are lightly coated.

HERSHEY'S WHITE AND DARK CHOCOLATE FUDGE TORTE

1 cup (2 sticks) butter or margarine,
   melted
1½ cups sugar
1 teaspoon vanilla extract
3 eggs, separated
⅔ cup HERSHEY'S Cocoa
½ cup all-purpose flour

3 tablespoons water
1⅔ cups (10-oz. pkg.) HERSHEY'S
   Vanilla Milk Chips, divided
⅛ teaspoon cream of tartar
SATINY GLAZE (recipe follows)
WHITE DECORATOR DRIZZLE
   (recipe follows)

Line bottom of 9-inch springform pan with foil; butter foil and side of pan. Heat oven to 350°F. In large mixer bowl, combine melted butter, sugar and vanilla; beat well. Add egg yolks, one at a time, beating well after each addition. Blend in cocoa, flour and water; beat well. Stir in 1⅓ cups vanilla milk chips. In small mixer bowl, beat egg whites and cream of tartar until stiff peaks form; carefully fold into chocolate mixture. Pour into prepared pan. Bake 45 minutes or until top begins to crack slightly. (Cake will not test done in center.) Cool 1 hour. Cover; refrigerate until firm. Remove side of pan. Pour SATINY GLAZE over cake; spread glaze evenly on top and side. Decorate top of torte with WHITE DECORATOR DRIZZLE. Cover; refrigerate until serving time. 10 to 12 servings.

SATINY GLAZE: In small microwave-safe bowl, place 1 cup HERSHEY'S Semi-Sweet Chocolate Chips and ¼ cup whipping cream. Microwave at HIGH (100%) 1 minute or just until chocolate is melted and mixture is smooth when stirred. Cool to lukewarm and slightly thickened.

WHITE DECORATOR DRIZZLE: In small microwave-safe bowl, place remaining ⅓ cup vanilla milk chips and 2 teaspoons shortening. Microwave at HIGH (100%) 20 to 30 seconds or just until chips are melted and mixture is smooth when stirred. Drizzle with spoon or place in pastry bag with writing tip.

CHOCOLATE CHUNKS PEANUT BUTTER COFFEECAKE

1⅔ cups (10-oz. pkg.) REESE'S
   Peanut Butter Chips, divided
2 tablespoons shortening
2¼ cups all-purpose flour
1½ cups packed light brown sugar
½ cup (1 stick) butter or margarine,
   softened

1 teaspoon baking powder
½ teaspoon baking soda
1 cup milk
3 eggs
1 teaspoon vanilla extract
1¾ cups (10-oz. pkg.) HERSHEY'S
   Semi-Sweet Chocolate Chunks

Heat oven to 350°F. Grease bottom of 13x9x2 baking pan. In medium microwave-safe bowl, place peanut butter chips and shortening. Microwave at HIGH (100%) 1½ to 2 minutes or until chips are melted when stirred; set aside. In large mixer bowl, place flour, brown sugar, butter and peanut butter chip mixture. Beat on low speed of electric mixer until mixture resembles small crumbs; reserve 1 cup crumbs. To crumb mixture in mixer bowl, add baking powder, baking soda, milk, eggs and vanilla; beat until well combined. Pour into prepared pan; sprinkle top evenly with reserved crumbs. Bake 35 to 40 minutes or until wooden pick inserted in center comes out clean. Remove from oven to wire rack; immediately sprinkle chocolate chunks evenly over top. Cool completely. 12 to 16 servings.

HERSHEY'S SEMI-SWEET CHOCOLATE TORTE

6 bars (6 oz.) HERSHEY'S Semi-
Sweet Baking Chocolate, broken
into pieces
¾ cup (1½ sticks) butter or
margarine, softened
1½ cups sugar
2 eggs
2 teaspoons vanilla extract

2¼ cups all-purpose flour
1 teaspoon baking soda
½ teaspoon salt
1¼ cups water
CHOCOLATE CREAM FILLING
(recipe follows)
SEMI-SWEET ROYAL GLAZE (recipe
follows) OR 2 cups frosting

Heat oven to 350°F. Grease two 9-inch round baking pans. Line bottoms with wax paper; grease and flour paper and sides of pans. In small microwave-safe bowl, place chocolate. Microwave at HIGH (100%) 1 to 1½ minutes or until melted and smooth when stirred; cool to lukewarm. In large mixer bowl, beat butter and sugar until well blended; add eggs and vanilla, beating well. Blend in chocolate. Stir together flour, baking soda and salt; add alternately with water to butter mixture, beating until well blended. Pour batter evenly into prepared pans. Bake 30 to 35 minutes or until wooden pick inserted in center comes out clean. Cool 10 minutes; remove from pans to wire racks. Cool completely. Prepare CHOCOLATE CREAM FILLING. Spread filling between cake layers, with rounded side up on top layer; refrigerate. Prepare SEMI-SWEET ROYAL GLAZE. Pour over top allowing to run down sides; spread evenly over top and sides of torte. Cover; refrigerate. About 12 servings.

CHOCOLATE CREAM FILLING

2 bars (2 oz.) HERSHEY'S Semi-
Sweet Baking Chocolate
¼ cup milk
1 package (3 oz.) cream cheese,
softened

1 cup (½ pt.) cold whipping cream
¼ cup powdered sugar
1 teaspoon vanilla extract

In small saucepan over very low heat, melt chocolate with milk, stirring until mixture is smooth and well blended; cool slightly. In small mixer bowl, beat cream cheese until fluffy; gradually blend in chocolate mixture. In separate bowl, beat whipping cream, powdered sugar and vanilla until stiff; fold into chocolate mixture. Refrigerate until firm.

SEMI-SWEET ROYAL GLAZE: In small saucepan over very low heat, melt 8 bars (8 oz.) HERSHEY'S Semi-Sweet Baking Chocolate, stirring constantly, just until chocolate is melted and mixture is smooth. Remove from heat; cool until thickened and lukewarm, about 15 minutes.

HERSHEY BAR-COOKIE TORTE

1/3 cup butter or margarine, softened
3/4 cup sugar
1/2 cup packed light brown sugar
1 egg
1 teaspoon vanilla extract
2 1/2 cups all-purpose flour
1 teaspoon baking soda

1/2 teaspoon baking powder
1/2 teaspoon salt
1/2 cup buttermilk or sour milk*
HERSHEY BAR CREAM FILLING
    (recipe follows)
GLOSSY HERSHEY BAR GLAZE
    (recipe follows)

Heat oven to 375°F. LIghtly grease cookie sheet. In large mixer bowl, beat butter, granulated sugar and brown sugar until well blended. Add egg and vanilla; blend well. Stir together flour, baking soda, baking powder and salt; add alternately with buttermilk to butter mixture. Pour batter by level 1/2 cupfuls onto prepared cookie sheet (2 cookies per sheet). With spatula, spread evenly into 6-inch circles, 3 inches apart. Bake 7 to 8 minutes or until lightly browned. Remove from cookie sheet to wire rack. Cool completely. Refrigerate until ready to fill. Prepare HERSHEY BAR CREAM FILLING. Place one cookie on serving plate; spread with 1/2 cup HERSHEY BAR CREAM FILLING. Repeat layering with remaining cookies and filling, ending with a cookie. Spoon GLOSSY HERSHEY BAR GLAZE over top of torte. Refrigerate. 8 to 10 servings.

* To sour milk: Use 1 1/2 teaspoons white vinegar plus milk to equal 1/2 cup.

HERSHEY BAR CREAM FILLING

1 teaspoon unflavored gelatin
1/4 cup cold water

2 HERSHEY'S Milk Chocolate Bars
    (7 oz. each.), divided
1 cup (1/2 pt.) cold whipping cream

Sprinkle gelatin over cold water in small saucepan; let stand 2 minutes to soften. Cook over low heat, stirring constantly, until gelatin is dissolved. Remove from heat; add 1 1/2 chocolate bars, broken into pieces (reserve remaining half bar for glaze). Stir until chocolate is completely melted. (If necessary, melt over low heat.) Transfer mixture to medium bowl. Cool to lukewarm, about 10 minutes. In small mixer bowl, beat whipping cream until stiff; gradually fold whipped cream into chocolate mixture, blending carefully. Refrigerate about 1 hour or until filling begins to set. About 3 cups filling.

GLOSSY HERSHEY BAR GLAZE: In small microwave-safe bowl, place reserved chocolate bar half and 1 tablespoon water. Microwave at HIGH (100%) until chocolate is melted and smooth when stirred. Add additional water, if needed, until glaze is of spreading consistency.

SPECIAL DARK BANANA MUFFINS

1 package (about 14 oz.) banana
    quick bread mix
1 HERSHEY'S SPECIAL DARK
    Chocolate Bar (7 oz.), broken into
    pieces

3/4 cup chopped nuts
Powdered sugar

Heat oven to 350°F. Paper-line 24 muffin cups (2 1/2-inches in diameter). In large bowl, prepare quick bread batter according to package directions for loaf with water, vegetable oil and eggs. In medium microwave-safe bowl, place chocolate pieces. Microwave at HIGH (100%) 1 to 1 1/2 minutes or until chocolate is melted when stirred; stir into batter with nuts. Fill each muffin cup 2/3 full with batter. Bake 20 to 25 minutes or until wooden pick inserted in center comes out clean. Cool slightly; sprinkle with powdered sugar. Serve warm or at room temperature. About 24 muffins.

REESE'S PEANUT BUTTER AND HERSHEY'S KISSES TORTE

½ cup (1 stick) butter or margarine,
   softened
2 cups sugar
1 cup REESE'S Creamy or Crunchy
   Peanut Butter
1 teaspoon vanilla extract
3 eggs
2 cups all-purpose flour
1 teaspoon baking powder

½ teaspoon salt
1 cup buttermilk or sour milk*
1 cup flaked coconut
HERSHEY'S KISSES GANACHE
   (recipe follows)
FLUFFY REESE'S PEANUT BUTTER
   FROSTING (page 12)
Additional HERSHEY'S KISSES
   Chocolates, unwrapped (optional)

Heat oven to 350°F. Grease and flour three 9-inch round baking pans. In large mixer bowl, beat butter, sugar, peanut butter and vanilla until well blended. Add eggs, one at a time, beating well after each addition. Stir together flour, baking powder and salt; add alternately with buttermilk to butter mixture, beating until smooth and well blended. Stir in coconut. Pour batter into prepared pans. Bake 30 to 35 minutes or until wooden pick inserted in center comes out clean. Cool 10 minutes; remove from pans to wire racks. Cool completely. Prepare HERSHEY'S KISSES GANACHE. Spread cake layer with ½ cup ganache; top with second cake layer. Repeat procedure ending with plain layer on top. Frost torte with FLUFFY REESE'S PEANUT BUTTER FROSTING. Garnish with additional chocolate pieces, if desired. Refrigerate leftovers. 10 to 12 servings.

*To sour milk: Use 1 tablespoon white vinegar plus milk to equal 1 cup.

HERSHEY'S KISSES GANACHE: In small saucepan, heat 8 ounces (about 44) unwrapped HERSHEY'S KISSES Chocolates and ⅓ cup whipping cream. Remove from heat. Add 1½ teaspoons softened butter or margarine and 1 teaspoon vanilla extract; stir until smooth. Refrigerate until firm enough to spread, about 1 hour. About 1 cup ganache.

EASY PEANUT BUTTER AND JELLY COFFEECAKE

2 cups all-purpose biscuit baking mix
2 tablespoons sugar
1 egg
⅔ cup milk

2 tablespoons vegetable oil
1½ cups REESE'S Peanut Butter
   Chips, divided
½ cup jelly or preserves

Heat oven to 400°F. Grease 9-inch square baking pan. In large mixer bowl, combine baking mix, sugar, egg, milk and oil; beat until smooth, about ½ minute. Stir in 1 cup peanut butter chips. Spread batter into prepared pan. Bake 20 to 25 minutes or until wooden pick inserted in center comes out clean. Remove from oven; immediately spread with jelly. Sprinkle remaining ½ cup peanut butter chips over top. Serve warm or cool. About 9 servings.

CREME DE CACAO TORTE

⅔ cup butter or margarine, softened
1⅔ cups sugar
3 eggs
½ teaspoon vanilla extract
2 cups all-purpose flour
⅔ cup HERSHEY'S Cocoa
1¼ teaspoons baking soda
¼ teaspoon baking powder

1⅓ cups milk
2 tablespoons creme de cacao
   (chocolate-flavored liqueur)
   (optional)
CREME DE CACAO FILLING (recipe
   follows)
CHOCOLATE GANACHE GLAZE
   (recipe follows)

Heat oven to 350°F. Grease and flour two 9-inch round baking pans. In large mixer bowl, beat butter, sugar, eggs and vanilla until blended. Stir together flour, cocoa, baking soda and baking powder; add to butter mixture alternately with milk, blending just until combined. Pour batter into prepared pans. Bake 30 to 35 minutes or until wooden pick inserted in center comes out clean. Cool 10 minutes; remove from pans to wire racks. Sprinkle each layer with 1 tablespoon creme de cacao; cool completely. Meanwhile, prepare CREME DE CACAO FILLING. Split each cake layer horizontally into 2 layers. Place one layer on serving plate; spread with one-third of FILLING. Repeat layering with remaining cake and FILLING, ending with cake layer. Cover tightly; refrigerate at least 8 hours. Prepare CHOCOLATE GANACHE GLAZE; spoon on top of chilled cake, allowing glaze to drizzle down side of cake. Refrigerate. 10 to 12 servings.

CREME DE CACAO FILLING: In small mixer bowl, beat 1 cup (½ pt.) cold whipping cream, 2 tablespoons creme de cacao and 1 tablespoon HERSHEY'S Cocoa until stiff. Cover; refrigerate. About 2 cups.

CHOCOLATE GANACHE GLAZE

1 HERSHEY'S SPECIAL DARK
   Chocolate Bar (7 oz.), broken into
   pieces
¼ cup whipping cream

1 tablespoon butter
1½ teaspoons creme de cacao
   (chocolate-flavored liqueur)

In medium saucepan, combine chocolate bar pieces, whipping cream and butter; cook over low heat, stirring constantly, until mixture is melted and smooth. Stir in creme de cacao. Cool to lukewarm (glaze will be slightly thickened). About 1 cup.

BUTTERSCOTCH STREUSEL MUFFIN TOPS

1⅔ cups (10-oz. pkg.) HERSHEY'S
   Butterscotch Chips, divided
2 tablespoons butter or margarine
3 cups all-purpose flour, divided
1 cup sugar
1½ teaspoons baking powder

½ teaspoon baking soda
½ teaspoon ground cinnamon
1 cup chopped nuts (optional)
⅔ cup milk
¼ cup vegetable oil
1 egg, slightly beaten

Heat oven to 350°F. Lightly grease cookie sheet. In medium microwave-safe bowl, place ⅔ cup butterscotch chips and butter. Microwave at HIGH (100%) 45 to 60 seconds or until chips are melted and mixture is smooth when stirred. Add ¾ cup flour; blend until mixture forms crumbs. Set aside. In large mixing bowl, stir together remaining 2¼ cups flour, remaining 1 cup chips, sugar, baking powder, baking soda, cinnamon and nuts, if desired. In separate bowl, stir together milk, oil and egg; add all at once to flour mixture. Stir until just moistened (batter should be lumpy). Spoon batter in 2-tablespoon-size mounds 2 inches apart on prepared cookie sheet. Sprinkle reserved crumb mixture evenly over muffin tops. Bake 10 to 12 minutes or until golden brown. Cool slightly; remove from cookie sheet. Serve warm. About 20 muffin tops.

CHOCOLATE CHIP PEANUT BUTTER MUFFINS

2 cups all-purpose flour
1 cup HERSHEY'S MINI CHIPS
   Semi-Sweet Chocolate
1 teaspoon baking powder
1/2 teaspoon baking soda
1/4 teaspoon salt
1 cup sugar
1 cup REESE'S Creamy Peanut Butter

1/4 cup (1/2 stick) butter or margarine,
   melted
2 eggs
1 cup milk
1 teaspoon vanilla extract
SUGAR GLAZE (recipe follows)

Heat oven to 400°F. Paper-line 24 muffin cups (2 1/2 inches in diameter). In large bowl, stir together flour, chocolate chips, baking powder, baking soda and salt; set aside. Stir together sugar, peanut butter, butter and eggs. Add milk and vanilla; stir until well blended. Add all at once to flour mixture; stir until just moistened. Fill muffin cups about 3/4 full. Bake 15 minutes or until lightly browned. Cool 5 minutes. Meanwhile, prepare SUGAR GLAZE. Drizzle over cupcakes. Serve warm or cool. About 2 dozen cupcakes.

SUGAR GLAZE: In small bowl, stir together 1/2 cup powdered sugar and 2 to 3 teaspoons warm water; stir until smooth and of desired consistency. Additional powdered sugar or water may be added if necessary. About 1/4 cup glaze.

MINI CHIP STREUSEL COFFEECAKE

STREUSEL (recipe follows)
1/2 cup (1 stick) butter or margarine,
   softened
1 cup sugar
3 eggs
1 teaspoon vanilla extract

1 cup (8 oz.) dairy sour cream
2 cups all-purpose flour
1 teaspoon baking powder
1 teaspoon baking soda
1/4 cup HERSHEY'S MINI CHIPS
   Semi-Sweet Chocolate

Heat oven to 350°F. Grease well and flour 12-cup fluted tube pan. Prepare STREUSEL; set aside. In large mixer bowl, beat butter and sugar until creamy. Add eggs; blend on low speed of electric mixer. Stir in vanilla and sour cream. Stir together flour, baking powder and baking soda; add to batter, stirring until well mixed. Sprinkle 1 cup reserved STREUSEL without chocolate chips into prepared pan. Spread one-third batter (about 1 1/2 cups) in pan; sprinkle with 1 cup STREUSEL. Repeat layers; end with batter on top. Bake 55 to 60 minutes or until wooden pick inserted in center comes out clean. Let stand 10 minutes; with knife, loosen cake from pan. Invert cake onto serving plate. Cool thoroughly. In small microwave-safe bowl, place small chocolate chips. Microwave at HIGH (100%) 30 seconds to 1 minute or until chips are melted and smooth when stirred. Drizzle over cake. 10 to 12 servings.

STREUSEL

3/4 cup packed brown sugar
1/4 cup (1/2 stick) butter or margarine,
   softened
1/4 cup all-purpose flour
1/4 teaspoon salt

1/4 teaspoon ground cinnamon
1 cup chopped walnuts
3/4 cup HERSHEY'S MINI CHIPS
   Semi-Sweet Chocolate

In small bowl, stir together brown sugar, butter, flour, salt and cinnamon; stir until crumbly. Stir in nuts. Reserve one cup of streusel for bottom of pan. Stir small chocolate chips into remaining streusel.

PIES

YANKEE DOODLE CHOCOLATE PIE

3½ cups (8 oz.) frozen non-dairy
whipped topping, thawed
1 cup HERSHEY'S Chocolate Fudge
Topping (room temperature)
¼ cup milk

1 packaged chocolate flavored crumb
crust (6 oz.)
Additional HERSHEY'S Chocolate
Fudge Topping, warmed

In small mixer bowl, combine whipped topping, fudge topping and milk; beat at low speed of electric mixer until blended, about 1 minute. Spoon into crust. Cover; freeze overnight. Serve with additional warm fudge topping; decorate as desired. About 6 servings.

FROZEN PEANUT BUTTER PIE

½ cup REESE'S Creamy Peanut
Butter
1 package (3 oz.) cream cheese,
softened
½ teaspoon vanilla extract
1 cup powdered sugar

½ cup milk
3½ cups (8 oz.) frozen non-dairy
whipped topping, thawed
1 packaged graham cracker crumb
crust (6 oz.)

In small mixer bowl, combine peanut butter, cream cheese and vanilla; beat until smooth. Gradually add powdered sugar and milk, blending until smooth. Fold in topping. Pour into crust. Freeze several hours or until firm. 6 to 8 servings.

PISTACHIO RUM PIE

5 bars (5 oz.) HERSHEY'S Semi-
Sweet Baking Chocolate, broken
into pieces
½ cup whipping cream
1 baked 9-inch pie crust, cooled

⅓ cup chopped, unsalted pistachio
nuts
1 package (6 serving size) vanilla
pudding and pie filling
2½ cups milk
1 teaspoon rum extract

In small microwave-safe bowl, place chocolate and whipping cream. Microwave at HIGH (100%) 1 to 1½ minutes or until chocolate is melted and mixture is smooth when stirred. Pour into crust; spread evenly over bottom. Sprinkle pistachios over chocolate; cool. Meanwhile, cook pudding according to package directions with 2½ cups milk; remove from heat. Stir in rum extract, blending well; carefully pour over chocolate mixture in crust. Press plastic wrap directly onto surface; refrigerate until firm. 8 servings.

EASY CHOCOLATE PEPPERMINT PIE

1 packaged crumb crust (6 oz.)
12 small (1½ inch) YORK Peppermint
Patties, unwrapped and quartered

2 tablespoons milk
3½ cups (8 oz.) frozen non-dairy
whipped topping, thawed*

In medium microwave-safe bowl, place peppermint pattie pieces and milk. Microwave at HIGH 1 minute or just until mixture is melted and smooth when stirred. Cool slightly. Fold whipped topping into melted chocolate; spoon into crust. Cover; freeze several hours or until firm. Garnish as desired. 6 to 8 servings.

* NOTE: Do not use "extra creamy" or "light" whipped topping.

BLACK BOTTOM PEANUT BUTTER PIE

¼ cup HERSHEY'S Semi-Sweet
  Chocolate Chips
1 cup (½ pt.) whipping cream, divided
1 baked 9-inch pie crust
¾ cup sugar
1 teaspoon cornstarch
½ teaspoon unflavored gelatin

1 cup milk
2 eggs
1½ teaspoons vanilla extract
¾ cup REESE'S Creamy Peanut
  Butter
Sweetened whipped cream (optional)
Chocolate curls (optional)

In small microwave-safe bowl, place chocolate chips and 3 tablespoons whipping cream. Microwave at HIGH (100%) 1 minute or until chips are melted and mixture is smooth when stirred. Spread chocolate mixture over bottom of pie crust; refrigerate 30 minutes or until firm. Meanwhile, in medium saucepan, stir together sugar, cornstarch and gelatin, set aside. Stir together milk, eggs and vanilla. Gradually blend into sugar mixture. Cook over medium-low heat, stirring constantly, until mixture thickens and boils. Boil, stirring constantly, 1 minute. Remove from heat. Add peanut butter; stir until smooth. Cool to room temperature. In small mixer bowl, beat remaining whipping cream until stiff; gradually fold into peanut butter mixture. Spread mixture over chocolate layer in pie crust. Refrigerate several hours or until firm. Garnish with sweetened whipped cream and chocolate curls, if desired. 8 servings.

SECRET CHOCOLATE STRAWBERRY PIE

3 cups sliced fresh strawberries (about
  2½ pints), divided
1 cup sugar
2 teaspoons cornstarch
1 package (3 oz.) strawberry flavored
  gelatin
1 tablespoon butter or margarine
1 tablespoon lemon juice

¼ cup HERSHEY'S Semi-Sweet
  Chocolate Chips
4 tablespoons whipping cream,
  divided
1 baked 9-inch pie crust, cooled
1 package (3 oz.) cream cheese,
  softened
Sweetened whipped cream (optional)
Whole strawberries (optional)

Reserve 2 cups strawberries; set aside. Mash remaining strawberries; add enough water to make 2 cups. In medium saucepan, stir together sugar and cornstarch; stir in mashed strawberries. Cook over medium heat, stirring constantly, until mixture comes to a boil; cook 2 minutes, stirring constantly. Remove from heat. Add gelatin, butter and lemon juice; stir until gelatin in dissolved. Refrigerate until partially set. Meanwhile, in small microwave-safe bowl, place chocolate chips and 3 tablespoons whipping cream. Microwave at HIGH (100%) 1 minute or until chips are melted and mixture is smooth when stirred. Spread chocolate mixture over bottom of pie crust; refrigerate 30 minutes or until firm. In small mixer bowl, beat remaining 1 tablespoon whipping cream into cream cheese; spread over chocolate layer. Refrigerate filled crust while gelatin mixture is cooling. When gelatin mixture is partially set, fold in reserved sliced strawberries; spoon mixture over cream cheese layer in pie shell. Refrigerate several hours or until firm. Serve with sweetened whipped cream and additional strawberries, if desired. 8 servings.

CHOCOLATE RUM MOUSSE PIE

1 teaspoon unflavored gelatin
1 tablespoon cold water
2 tablespoons boiling water
½ cup sugar
⅓ cup HERSHEY'S European Style
  Cocoa

1 cup (½ pt.) cold whipping cream
1 teaspoon vanilla extract
1 baked 8- or 9-inch pie crust, cooled
RUM CREAM TOPPING (recipe
  follows)

In small cup, sprinkle gelatin over cold water; let stand 1 minute to soften. Add boiling water; stir until gelatin is completely dissolved and mixture is clear. Cool slightly, about 5 minutes. Meanwhile, in small mixer bowl, stir together sugar and cocoa; add whipping cream and vanilla. Beat on medium speed of electric mixer, scraping bottom of bowl occasionally, until stiff; pour in gelatin mixture and beat just until well blended. Pour mixture into pie crust. Spread RUM CREAM TOPPING over chocolate. Refrigerate at least 2 hours. 6 to 8 servings.

RUM CREAM TOPPING: In small mixer bowl, beat 1 cup (½ pt.) cold whipping cream, 2 tablespoons powdered sugar and 2 teaspoons light rum or ½ teaspoon rum extract until stiff.

FESTIVE FROZEN PEANUT BUTTER PECAN PIE

1 cup chopped pecans
1 tablespoon plus 1½ teaspoons butter
  or margarine
1⅔ cups (10-oz. pkg.) REESE'S
  Peanut Butter Chips
½ cup milk
2 packages (3 oz.) cream cheese,
  softened

⅔ cup powdered sugar
1 envelope (1.3 oz.) whipped topping
  mix
1 packaged crumb crust (6 oz.)
PEANUT BUTTER SAUCE (recipe
  follows)

Heat oven to 325°F. Place pecans and butter in baking pan, toast in oven about 7 minutes, stirring occasionally, until butter is melted and nuts are coated; set aside to cool. Meanwhile, in medium microwave-safe bowl, place peanut butter chips and milk. Microwave at HIGH (100%) 1 minute; stir. If necessary, microwave an additional 15 seconds at a time, stirring after each heating, just until chips are melted when stirred; cool 10 minutes. In large mixer bowl, beat cream cheese and powdered sugar until fluffy; blend in peanut butter mixture. Prepare whipped topping mix according to package directions; fold in peanut butter mixture and ½ cup toasted pecans. Pour into crust. Wrap tightly; freeze several hours. Serve with warm PEANUT BUTTER SAUCE; garnish with remaining pecans. 6 to 8 servings.

PEANUT BUTTER SAUCE

1 cup REESE'S Peanut Butter chips
⅓ cup milk

¼ cup whipping cream
¼ teaspoon vanilla extract

In medium microwave-safe bowl, place peanut butter chips, milk and whipping cream. Microwave at HIGH (100%) 2 to 2½ minutes; stir. If necessary, microwave at HIGH an additional 30 seconds at a time, stirring after each heating, just until chips are melted when stirred. Stir in vanilla; serve warm. Refrigerate leftover sauce. About 1 cup sauce.

DUTCH APPLE BUTTERSCOTCH CRUMB PIE

4 cups peeled, thinly sliced apples
1 cup all-purpose flour, divided
¼ cup sugar
½ teaspoon ground cinnamon
1 baked 9-inch pie crust, cooled

1⅔ cups (10-oz. pkg.) HERSHEY'S
  Butterscotch Chips, divided
½ cup whipping cream
2 tablespoons butter or margarine

Heat oven to 375°F. In large bowl, toss apples, ¼ cup flour, sugar and cinnamon; spread in pie crust. In small microwave-safe bowl, place ⅔ cups butterscotch chips and whipping cream. Microwave at HIGH (100%) 1 to 1½ minutes or until chips are melted and mixture is smooth when stirred vigorously. Pour mixture over apples; set aside. In medium microwave-safe bowl, place remaining 1 cup chips and butter. Microwave at HIGH 1 to 1½ minutes or until chips are melted and mixture is smooth when stirred vigorously. Add remaining ¾ cup flour; blend until mixture forms crumbs. Sprinkle crumbs over top. Bake 50 to 55 minutes or until apples are tender and surface is browned. To prevent excessive browning, cover pie with foil during last 20 minutes of baking. Serve warm or cool. 6 to 8 servings.

TRIPLE CHOCOLATE BROWNIE PIE

2 eggs
1 cup sugar
½ cup (1 stick) butter or margarine,
  melted
½ cup all-purpose flour
⅓ cup HERSHEY'S Cocoa
¼ teaspoon salt

½ cup HERSHEY'S Semi-Sweet
  Chocolate Chips
½ cup chopped nuts
1 teaspoon vanilla extract
Vanilla ice cream
HERSHEY'S Chocolate Shoppe
  Topping

Heat oven to 350°F. Grease 8-inch pie plate. In small mixer bowl, beat eggs; blend in sugar and butter. Stir together flour, cocoa and salt; add to egg mixture, beating until blended. Stir in chocolate chips, nuts and vanilla. Spread batter into prepared pie plate. Bake 35 minutes or until set (pie will not test done in center). Cool completely; cut into wedges. Serve with ice cream; top with topping. 6 to 8 servings.

Note: 9-inch pie plate may be used. Bake at 350°F. 30 minutes.

CREAMY PEANUT BUTTER PIE

1 package (3 oz.) cream cheese,
  softened
1 teaspoon lemon juice
1 cup REESE'S Peanut Butter Chips
⅔ cup sweetened condensed milk

½ cup cold whipping cream
1 packaged graham cracker crumb
  crust (6 oz.)
WHIPPED CREAM TOPPING (recipe
  follows)

In small mixer bowl, beat cream cheese and lemon juice on medium speed of electric mixer until fluffy, about 2 minutes; set aside. In top of double boiler over hot water, melt peanut butter chips with sweetened condensed milk. Add warm peanut butter mixture to cream cheese mixture. Beat on medium speed until blended, about 1 minute. In small mixer bowl, beat whipping cream until stiff; fold into peanut butter mixture. Pour into crust. Cover; refrigerate several hours or overnight. Prepare WHIPPED CREAM TOPPING; spread over filling just before serving. Refrigerate leftovers. 6 to 8 servings.

WHIPPED CREAM TOPPING: In small mixer bowl, combine ½ cup cold whipping cream, 1 tablespoon powdered sugar and 1 teaspoon vanilla extract; beat until stiff.

EASIEST EVER FROSTY CHOCOLATE PIE

1¼ cups HERSHEY'S Hot Fudge
Chocolate Shoppe Topping,
divided

3½ cups (8 oz.) frozen non-dairy
whipped topping, thawed
1 packaged chocolate flavored crumb
crust (6 oz.)

In medium bowl, stir together 1 cup fudge topping and whipped topping until well blended; spread into prepared crust. In small microwave-safe bowl, place remaining ¼ cup fudge topping. Microwave at HIGH (100%) 15 to 30 seconds or just until warm; drop by spoonfuls on top of pie; with knife or metal spatula, draw through dollops for marbled effect. Cover; freeze until firm. Cut into slices; serve cold. Cover and freeze leftovers. About 8 servings.

FLAVOR VARIATIONS: Since thicknesses of fudge topping vary, follow the directions below for your favorite flavor HERSHEY'S Chocolate Shoppe Topping in pie; place pie in freezer. After pie begins to freeze, drop remaining amount listed below of fudge topping by dollops on pie; swirl, store and freeze as directed above.

BANANA SPLIT FUDGE: Use ⅓ cup for pie; use ¼ cup for top.

BUTTERSCOTCH CARAMEL FUDGE: Use ⅓ cup for pie; use 2 tablespoons for top.

CHOCOLATE CARAMEL FUDGE: Use ⅓ cup for pie; use 2 tablespoons for top.

CHOCOLATE ALMOND FUDGE: Use ½ cup for pie; use ¼ cup for top.

DOUBLE CHOCOLATE FUDGE: Use ¾ cup for pie; use ¼ cup for top.

SPECIAL DARK TARTS

1 HERSHEY'S SPECIAL DARK
Chocolate Bar (7 oz.), broken into
pieces
⅓ cup milk
1⅓ cups miniature marshmallows

1 cup (½ pt.) cold whipping cream,
divided
8 single serve graham cracker crusts
2 teaspoons powdered sugar
¼ teaspoon vanilla extract

In small saucepan over very low heat, melt chocolate with milk, stirring constantly, until smooth. Add marshmallows; stir until smooth. Remove from heat; cool completely. In small mixer bowl, beat ⅔ cup whipping cream until stiff; fold into chocolate mixture. Divide evenly into crusts. Cover; refrigerate until firm. Just before serving, beat remaining ⅓ cup whipping cream, powdered sugar and vanilla until stiff; serve on tarts as garnish. Refrigerate leftovers. 8 servings.

CHOCOLATE AND STRAWBERRY RIBBON PIE

1 cup HERSHEY'S Semi-Sweet
Chocolate Chips
3 tablespoons light cream
1 package (10 oz.) frozen strawberries
in syrup, thawed and drained

3½ cups (8 oz.) frozen non-dairy
whipped topping, thawed and
divided
1 packaged chocolate flavored crumb
crust (6 oz.)

In medium microwave-safe bowl, place chocolate chips and light cream. Microwave at HIGH (100%) 1 to 1½ minutes or until chocolate is melted and mixture is smooth when stirred. Set aside; cool to lukewarm. Drain strawberries; puree to equal ⅔ cup. In small bowl, fold together 2 cups whipped topping and strawberry puree. Spread half of strawberry mixture on bottom of crust. Combine chocolate with remaining 1½ cups whipped topping; carefully spoon over strawberry mixture in crust. Top with remaining strawberry mixture. Cover; freeze until firm. Allow to soften 5 minutes before serving. 8 servings.

BRANDY ALEXANDER PIE

30 large marshmallows
½ cup milk
1 cup HERSHEY'S Semi-Sweet
    Chocolate Chips
1 teaspoon vanilla extract
1 to 2 tablespoons brandy

1 to 2 tablespoons creme de cacao
    (chocolate-flavored liqueur)
2 cups (1 pt.) cold whipping cream
CHOCOLATE PETAL CRUST (recipe
    follows)

In medium saucepan, combine marshmallows and milk; cook over low heat, stirring constantly, until marshmallows are melted and mixture is smooth. Into small bowl, pour half of marshmallow mixture (¾ cup); set aside. Add chocolate chips to remaining marshmallow mixture. Return to low heat; stir until chips are melted. Remove from heat; stir in vanilla. Cool to room temperature. Stir brandy and liqueur into reserved marshmallow mixture; refrigerate until mixture mounds slightly when dropped from a spoon. In small mixer bowl, beat whipping cream until stiff. Fold 2 cups whipped cream into cooled chocolate mixture; spoon into CHOCOLATE PETAL CRUST. Blend remaining whipped cream into chilled brandy mixture; spread over chocolate mixture. Refrigerate 2 hours or until firm. 8 servings.

CHOCOLATE PETAL CRUST

½ cup (1 stick) butter or margarine,
    softened
1 cup sugar
1 egg
1 teaspoon vanilla extract

1¼ cups all-purpose flour
½ cup HERSHEY'S Cocoa
¾ teaspoon baking soda
¼ teaspoon salt

In large mixer bowl, beat butter, sugar, egg and vanilla until blended. Stir together flour, cocoa, baking soda and salt; gradually beat into butter mixture. Shape soft dough into two 6½-inch rolls. Wrap in plastic wrap; refrigerate several hours. Heat oven to 375°F. Grease 9-inch pie plate. Cut one roll into ⅛-inch-thick slices; arrange slices, edges touching, on bottom, up side and onto rim of prepared pie plate. (Small spaces in crust will not affect pie.) Bake 8 to 10 minutes. Cool on wire rack.

Note: Remaining roll of dough may be frozen up to 6 weeks for later use.

CHOCOLATE CHIP WALNUT PIE

¾ cup packed light brown sugar
½ cup all-purpose flour
½ teaspoon baking powder
¼ teaspoon ground cinnamon
2 eggs, slightly beaten

1 cup HERSHEY'S Semi-Sweet
    Chocolate Chips, MINI CHIPS or
    Milk Chocolate Chips
1 cup coarsely chopped walnuts
1 baked 9-inch pie crust, cooled
SPICED CREAM (recipe follows)

Heat oven to 350°F. In bowl, stir together brown sugar, flour, baking powder and cinnamon. Add eggs; stir until well blended. Stir in chocolate chips and walnuts. Pour into baked pie crust. Bake 25 to 30 minutes or until lightly browned and set. Serve slightly warm or at room temperature with SPICED CREAM. 8 servings.

SPICED CREAM: In small mixer bowl, combine ½ cup cold whipping cream, 1 tablespoon powdered sugar, ¼ teaspoon vanilla extract, ¼ teaspoon ground cinnamon and dash ground nutmeg; beat until stiff. About 1 cup topping.

REESE'S PEANUT BUTTER AND HERSHEY'S KISSES LAYER PIE

18 HERSHEY'S KISSES Chocolates, unwrapped
1 cup (1/2 pt.) whipping cream, divided
1 baked 9-inch pie crust, cooled
1 package (6 serving size) vanilla pudding and pie filling mix*
2 cups milk

1/2 cup REESE'S Creamy Peanut Butter
1 tablespoon powdered sugar
1/4 teaspoon vanilla extract
Additional HERSHEY'S KISSES Chocolates, unwrapped (optional)

In small microwave-safe bowl, place chocolate pieces and 2 tablespoons whipping cream. Microwave at HIGH (100%) 1 minute or until chocolate is melted and mixture is smooth when stirred. Spread chocolate mixture over bottom of pie shell; refrigerate 30 minutes or until set. In 2-quart saucepan, place pudding mix and peanut butter. Using wire whisk, gradually blend in milk, stirring until smooth. Cook over medium heat, stirring constantly, until pudding thickens and boils; remove from heat. Cool 10 minutes; stirring frequently. Pour pudding over chocolate mixture in pie shell. Refrigerate several hours or until firm. In small mixer bowl, beat remaining whipping cream, powdered sugar and vanilla until stiff. Spread over top of pie. Garnish with additional milk chocolates, if desired. Cover and refrigerate leftovers. 8 servings.

* Do not use instant pudding mix.

VANILLA CHIP FRUIT TART

3/4 cup (1 1/2 sticks) butter or margarine, softened
1/2 cup powdered sugar

1 1/2 cups all-purpose flour
VANILLA FILLING (recipe follows)
FRUIT TOPPING (recipe follows)

Heat oven to 300°F. In small mixer bowl, beat butter and powdered sugar until smooth; blend in flour. Press mixture onto bottom and up side of 12-inch round pizza pan. Flute edge, if necessary. Bake 20 to 25 minutes or until lightly browned; cool completely. Prepare VANILLA FILLING; spread on cooled crust. Cover; refrigerate. Prepare FRUIT TOPPING. Cover; refrigerate assembled tart until just before serving. 10 to 12 servings.

VANILLA FILLING: In microwave-safe bowl, place 1 2/3 cups (10-oz.pkg.) HERSHEY'S Vanilla Milk Chips and 1/4 cup whipping cream. Microwave at HIGH (100%) 1 to 1 1/2 minutes or until chips are melted and mixture is smooth when stirred vigorously. Beat in 1 package (8 oz.) softened cream cheese.

FRUIT TOPPING

1/4 cup sugar
1 tablespoon cornstarch
1/2 cup pineapple juice

1/2 teaspoon lemon juice
Assorted fresh fruit, sliced

In small saucepan, stir together sugar and cornstarch; stir in juices. Cook over medium heat, stirring constantly, until thickened; cool. Meanwhile, arrange fruit on top of filling; carefully pour or brush juice mixture over fruit.

CHOCOLATE & VANILLA SWIRL TART

⅔ cup HERSHEY'S Semi-Sweet
  Chocolate Chips
½ cup milk, divided
2 tablespoons sugar
½ teaspoon unflavored gelatin
1 tablespoon cold water

⅔ cup HERSHEY'S Vanilla Milk
  Chips
1 teaspoon vanilla extract
1 cup (½ pt.) cold whipping cream
TART SHELL (recipe follows)

In small microwave-safe bowl, place chocolate chips, ¼ cup milk and sugar. Microwave at HIGH (100%) 1 minute or until hot. Stir or whisk until smooth; cool to room temperature. In small bowl, sprinkle gelatin over cold water; allow to stand 2 minutes to soften. In second small microwave-safe bowl, place vanilla chips and remaining ¼ cup milk. Microwave at HIGH 1 minute or until hot; stir or whisk until smooth. Add gelatin mixture and vanilla extract; stir until gelatin is dissolved. Cool to room temperature. In small mixer bowl, beat whipping cream until stiff; fold 1 cup into vanilla mixture. Fold chocolate mixture into remaining whipped cream. Alternately spoon chocolate and vanilla mixtures into baked tart shell; with spatula, swirl for marbled effect. Refrigerate until firm. 8 to 10 servings.

TART SHELL: Heat oven to 375°F. Grease bottom and sides of fluted 8 or 9-inch tart pan. In small mixer bowl, beat ½ cup softened butter or margarine and 2 tablespoons sugar until blended. Add 2 egg yolks, mixing well. Stir in 1 cup all-purpose flour until mixture is crumbly. Press onto bottom and up sides of prepared pan. (If dough is sticky, sprinkle with 1 tablespoon flour.) Prick bottom with fork to prevent puffing. Bake 8 to 10 minutes or until lightly browned. Cool completely.

EASY CHOCOLATE CHEESEPIE

2 bars (2 oz.) HERSHEY'S
  Unsweetened Baking Chocolate,
  broken into pieces
¼ cup (½ stick) butter or margarine,
  softened
¾ cup sugar
1 package (3 oz.) cream cheese,
  softened

1 teaspoon milk
2 cups frozen non-dairy whipped
  topping, thawed
1 packaged crumb crust (6 oz.)
Additional whipped topping (optional)

In small microwave-safe bowl, place chocolate. Microwave at HIGH (100%) 1 to 1½ minutes or until chocolate is melted and smooth when stirred; set aside. In small mixer bowl, beat butter, sugar, cream cheese and milk until well blended and smooth. Blend in chocolate. Gradually blend in whipped topping. Spoon into crust. Refrigerate until firm. Serve with additional whipped topping, if desired. 6 to 8 servings.

PEANUT BUTTER CREAM PIE

1 package (4 serving size) instant
  vanilla pudding and pie filling
1 cup (8 oz.) dairy sour cream
1 cup milk

1½ cups REESE'S Peanut Butter
  Chips
2 tablespoons vegetable oil
1 packaged crumb crust (6 oz.)
Whipped topping

In small mixer bowl, blend pudding mix, sour cream and milk; set aside. In small microwave-safe bowl, place peanut butter chips and oil. Microwave at HIGH (100%) 45 seconds; stir. If necessary, microwave at HIGH additional 15 seconds or until melted and smooth when stirred. Gradually add to pudding, blending well. Pour into crust. Cover; refrigerate several hours or overnight. Garnish with whipped topping. 6 to 8 servings.

MICROWAVE HERSHEY BAR PIE

1 HERSHEY'S Milk Chocolate Bar (7 oz.), broken into pieces
1/3 cup milk
1 1/2 cups miniature marshmallows
1 cup (1/2 pt.) cold whipping cream

CHOCOLATE CRUMB CRUST (recipe follows) or 1 baked 9-inch crumb crust
Sweetened whipped cream
Chilled cherry pie filling (optional)

In medium microwave-safe bowl, combine chocolate bar pieces, milk and marshmallows. Microwave at HIGH (100%) 1 1/2 to 2 1/2 minutes or until chocolate is softened and mixture is melted and smooth when stirred. Cool completely. In small mixer bowl, beat whipping cream until stiff; fold into chocolate mixture. Spoon into CHOCOLATE CRUMB CRUST. Cover; refrigerate several hours or until firm. Garnish with sweetened whipped cream; serve with chilled cherry pie filling, if desired. 8 servings.

CHOCOLATE CRUMB CRUST

1/2 cup (1 stick) butter or margarine
1 1/2 cups graham cracker crumbs

1/3 cup HERSHEY'S Cocoa
1/3 cup powdered sugar

Grease 9-inch microwave-safe pie plate. In small microwave-safe bowl, microwave butter at HIGH (100%) 1 minute or until melted. Stir in graham cracker crumbs, cocoa and powdered sugar until well blended. Press onto bottom and up side of prepared pie plate. Microwave an additional 1 to 1 1/2 minutes until bubbly. (Do not overcook.) Cool completely before filling.

PEANUT BUTTER SUNDAE PIE

1 quart vanilla ice cream
CHOCOLATE CRUMB CRUST (recipe follows)

PEANUT BUTTER CHIP ICE CREAM SAUCE (recipe follows)

Place scoops of ice cream into CHOCOLATE CRUMB CRUST. Cover; freeze until just before serving. Serve with PEANUT BUTTER CHIP ICE CREAM SAUCE. 8 servings.

CHOCOLATE CRUMB CRUST: In small bowl, combine 1 1/4 cups graham cracker crumbs, 1/4 cup HERSHEY'S Cocoa, 1/4 cup sugar and 1/3 cup melted butter or margarine. Press mixture onto bottom and up sides of buttered 9-inch pie plate. Cover; freeze.

PEANUT BUTTER CHIP ICE CREAM SAUCE

1 cup REESE'S Peanut Butter Chips
1/3 cup evaporated milk
2 tablespoons light corn syrup

1 tablespoon butter or margarine
1 teaspoon vanilla extract

In small microwave-safe bowl, combine peanut butter chips, evaporated milk, corn syrup and butter. Microwave at HIGH (100%) 1 to 1 1/2 minutes or until chips are softened; stir with wire whisk until chips are melted and mixture is smooth. If necessary, microwave at HIGH additional 30 seconds or until mixture is smooth when stirred. Cool slightly. About 3/4 cup sauce.

CONVENTIONAL DIRECTIONS: In small saucepan, combine all ingredients except vanilla. Cook over low heat, stirring constantly, until chips are melted and mixture is smooth. Stir in vanilla. Cool slightly.

STRAWBERRY CHIFFON PIE

1 package (3 oz.) strawberry flavored
   gelatin
¾ cup boiling water
2¼ cups fresh strawberries
2 cups frozen non-dairy whipped
   topping, thawed

½ cup HERSHEY'S Semi-Sweet
   Chocolate Chips
CHOCOLATE PASTRY (recipe
   follows)
1 teaspoon shortening

In medium bowl, dissolve gelatin in water; cool slightly. Set aside eight whole strawberries for garnish. Crush remaining berries or puree in food processor bowl (need ¾ cup puree). Stir strawberry puree into gelatin mixture; refrigerate until partially set (consistency of unbeaten egg whites). Fold whipped topping into strawberry mixture; spoon into CHOCOLATE PASTRY. Refrigerate 2 to 3 hours or until set. Meanwhile, prepare strawberries for garnish. In small microwave-safe bowl, place chocolate chips and shortening. Microwave at HIGH (100%) 1 to 1½ minutes or until chips are melted and smooth when stirred. Dip reserved strawberries into melted chocolate; place on wax paper-covered tray. Refrigerate, uncovered, about 30 minutes or until chocolate is firm. At serving time, garnish pie with the berries. Refrigerate leftovers. 8 servings.

CHOCOLATE PASTRY

1¼ cups all-purpose flour
¼ cup sugar
3 tablespoons HERSHEY'S Cocoa

¼ teaspoon salt
⅓ cup vegetable oil
3 tablespoons cold water

Stir together flour, sugar, cocoa and salt. In measuring cup, place oil; add water. Do not stir. Pour liquid over flour mixture; stir lightly with fork until well blended (if mixture is too dry, add 1 to 2 teaspoons additional cold water). With hands, press mixture into ball. Place between 2 pieces wax paper; roll into 12-inch circle. Peel off top sheet of paper. Gently invert pastry over 9-inch pie plate; peel off paper. Fit pastry into pie plate. Fold under extra pastry around edge; flute edge. With fork, prick bottom and sides of crust thoroughly. Refrigerate about ½ hour. Heat oven to 450°F. Bake 10 minutes. Cool thoroughly.

DESSERTS
BANANA ROYALE SUNDAE

½ cup HERSHEY'S Chocolate
   Shoppe Topping (any flavor)
2 ripe, large bananas
Vanilla ice cream

Sweetened whipped cream
Toasted sliced almonds*
Maraschino cherries (optional)

In large heavy skillet, heat topping until warm. Peel bananas; cut in half lengthwise and then in thirds crosswise. Add to skillet; cook, stirring constantly, just until warm. Spoon banana mixture over individual portions of ice cream. Garnish with whipped cream, almonds and cherry, if desired. Serve immediately. 4 servings.

   * To toast almonds: Heat oven to 350°F. Spread almonds in thin layer in shallow baking pan. Bake 8 to 10 minutes, stirring occasionally, until light golden brown: cool.

FRUITY PEANUT BUTTER CHIP CRUMBLE

1 can (21 oz.) apple, peach, apricot or
   blueberry pie filling
1 package (8 oz.) single layer yellow
   cake mix
1 cup REESE'S Peanut Butter Chips,
   divided

¼ cup (½ stick) butter or margarine,
   melted
Vanilla ice cream or frozen whipped
   topping, thawed (optional)

Heat oven to 375°F. Grease 8-inch square baking pan. Spread pie filling in prepared pan. Toss dry cake mix with ½ cup peanut butter chips; sprinkle over pie filling in pan. (Do not stir.) Spoon butter evenly over top, trying to moisten all cake mix. Bake 40 to 45 minutes or until golden brown. Remove from oven; immediately sprinkle with remaining ½ cup chips. Let stand 10 minutes. Serve with ice cream or whipped topping, if desired. 8 servings.

PEANUT BUTTER WASHINGTON SQUARES

1⅔ cups (10-oz. pkg.) REESE'S
   Peanut Butter Chips
½ cup (1 stick) butter or margarine
1 cup sugar
2 eggs
2 teaspoons vanilla extract

2 cups all-purpose flour
1½ teaspoons baking soda
½ teaspoon salt
1 can (21 oz.) cherry pie filling (or any
   other fruit flavor pie filling)
Vanilla ice cream

Heat oven to 375°F. In microwave-safe bowl, place peanut butter chips. Microwave at HIGH (100%) 1 minute; stir. If necessary, microwave at HIGH an additional 15 seconds at a time, stirring after each heating, just until chips are melted when stirred. In large mixer bowl, beat butter and sugar until light and fluffy. Add eggs and vanilla; beat well. Blend in melted chips. Stir together flour, baking soda and salt; add to butter mixture. Divide dough in half. Press one half onto bottom of ungreased 13x9x2-inch baking pan. Bake 10 minutes; set aside to cool. Meanwhile, cover and refrigerate remaining dough until stiff enough to handle, about 30 minutes. Pour pie filling evenly over baked layer. Roll remaining dough between 2 pieces of wax paper to form a ¼-inch-thick rectangle, 13x9 inches; cut into ½x13-inch strips. Lay strips, ½ inch apart, lattice-fashion, over pie filling in pan.* Bake 20 to 25 minutes or until browned. Serve warm with ice cream. About 12 servings.

   * Broken strips of dough may be pieced together and will mesh during baking.

HOT FUDGE PUDDING CAKE

1¼ cups granulated sugar, divided
1 cup all-purpose flour
7 tablespoons HERSHEY'S Cocoa,
    divided
2 teaspoons baking powder
¼ teaspoon salt

½ cup milk
⅓ cup butter or margarine, melted
1½ teaspoons vanilla extract
½ cup packed light brown sugar
1¼ cups hot water
Whipped topping

Heat oven to 350°F. In bowl, stir together ¾ cup granulated sugar, flour, 3 table-spoons cocoa, baking powder and salt. Stir in milk, butter and vanilla; beat until smooth. Pour batter into 8-or 9-inch square baking pan. Stir together remaining ½ cup granulated sugar, brown sugar and remaining 4 tablespoons cocoa; sprinkle mixture evenly over bat-ter. Pour hot water over top; do not stir. Bake 35 to 40 minutes or until center is almost set. Let stand 15 minutes; spoon into dessert dishes, spooning sauce from bottom of pan over top. Garnish with whipped topping, if desired. About 8 servings.

CHOCOLATE SHOPPE MOUSSE

1 teaspoon unflavored gelatin
1 tablespoon cold water
2 tablespoons boiling water
1 cup (½ pt.) cold whipping cream

½ cup of your favorite HERSHEY'S
    Chocolate Shoppe Topping, at
    room temperature

In small bowl, sprinkle gelatin over cold water; let stand 1 minute to soften. Add boiling water; stir until gelatin is completely dissolved and mixture is clear. Cool slightly. In small mixer bowl, on low speed of electric mixer, beat whipping cream and topping until well blended. Beat on medium speed, scraping bottom of bowl occasionally, until doubled in volume and thickened. Gradually pour in gelatin mixture; beating until well blended. Spoon into serving dishes. Refrigerate about ½ hour. Garnish as desired. Four ½ cup servings.

HERSHEY'S KISSES AND REESE'S PEANUT BUTTER SUNDAE

16 HERSHEY'S KISSES Chocolates,
    unwrapped
¼ cup water
½ cup REESE'S Creamy or Crunchy
    Peanut Butter
¼ cup light corn syrup

¼ teaspoon vanilla extract
Vanilla ice cream
Sweetened whipped cream
Additional HERSHEY'S KISSES
    Chocolates, unwrapped

Chop chocolate pieces into quarters; set aside. In small bowl, using wire whisk, gradually stir water into peanut butter until smooth. Add corn syrup and vanilla; blending until smooth. Spoon peanut butter sauce and chocolate pieces over individual servings of ice cream. Garnish with whipped cream and additional chocolate pieces. Serve immedi-ately. 6 to 8 servings.

MOCHA PUDDING CAKE

1¼ cups granulated sugar, divided
1 cup all-purpose flour
2 teaspoons baking powder
¼ teaspoon salt
½ cup (1 stick) butter or margarine
1 bar (1 oz.) HERSHEY'S
    Unsweetened Baking Chocolate

½ cup milk
1 teaspoon vanilla extract
½ cup packed light brown sugar
¼ cup HERSHEY'S Cocoa
1 cup hot strong coffee
Ice cream

Heat oven to 350°F. In bowl, stir together ¾ cup granulated sugar, flour, baking powder and salt. In small saucepan over low heat, melt butter with baking chocolate; add to dry ingredients with milk and vanilla. Beat until smooth. Pour batter into 8-or 9-inch square baking pan. Stir together remaining ½ cup granulated sugar, brown sugar and cocoa; sprinkle evenly over batter. Pour coffee over top; do not stir. Bake 35 to 40 minutes or until center is almost set. Let stand 15 minutes; spoon into dessert dishes, spooning sauce from bottom of pan over top. Serve with ice cream. About 8 servings.

CLASSIC CHOCOLATE PUDDING

2 bars (2 oz.) HERSHEY'S
    Unsweetened Baking Chocolate
2½ cups milk
1 cup sugar
¼ cup cornstarch

½ teaspoon salt
3 egg yolks, slightly beaten
1 tablespoon butter
1 teaspoon vanilla extract
Sweetened whipped cream (optional)

In medium saucepan, combine chocolate with 1½ cups milk; cook over low heat, stirring constantly with wire whisk, until chocolate is melted and mixture is smooth. In medium bowl, stir together sugar, cornstarch and salt; blend in remaining 1 cup milk and egg yolks. Gradually add to chocolate mixture, stirring constantly. Cook over medium heat, stirring constantly, until mixture boils; boil and stir 1 minute. Remove from heat; add butter and vanilla. Pour into bowl; press plastic wrap directly onto surface. Refrigerate. Serve topped with sweetened whipped cream. 4 to 6 servings.

PEANUT BUTTER AND BANANA PUDDING DESSERT

⅓ cup granulated sugar
2 tablespoons cornstarch
2 cups milk
2 egg yolks, slightly beaten
1⅔ cups (10 oz. pkg.) REESE'S
    Peanut Butter Chips, divided

2 tablespoons banana-flavored liqueur,
    optional
2 to 3 medium-size bananas, sliced ¼-
    inch thick

In 2-quart saucepan, combine sugar and cornstarch. Gradually stir in milk and egg yolks. Cook over medium heat, stirring constantly, until mixture begins to boil. Boil, stirring constantly, 1 minute. Remove from heat. Add 1½ cups peanut butter chips; stir until chips are melted and smooth. Stir in liqueur. Pour into bowl. Press plastic wrap directly onto surface of pudding. Cool to room temperature; refrigerate until cold. Place about ¼ cup pudding in each of four individual dishes. Place banana slices and remaining peanut butter chips on top of each dish of pudding. 8 servings.

FROZEN FUDGE SUNDAE DESSERT

2¼ cups finely crushed round buttery crackers (about 60 crackers)
½ cup (1 stick) butter or margarine, melted
1 jar (about 18 oz.) HERSHEY'S Chocolate Shoppe Topping (Banana Split Fudge, Butterscotch Caramel Fudge, Chocolate Caramel Fudge, Chocolate Almond Fudge, or Double Chocolate Fudge) *

2 packages (4 serving size) instant vanilla pudding and pie filling mix
1½ cups cold milk
4 cups (1 qt.) vanilla ice cream, slightly softened
3½ cups (8 oz.) frozen non-dairy whipped topping, thawed
12 to 15 maraschino cherries, drained (optional)

In 13x9x2-inch pan, stir together crushed crackers and butter; press onto bottom of pan. Carefully spread fudge topping over crumbs. In large bowl, stir together instant pudding mix, milk and ice cream until well blended; spread over mixture in pan. Top with whipped topping. Cover; freeze until firm, several hours or overnight. Serve frozen, cut into pieces; garnish each piece with maraschino cherry, if desired. Cover and freeze leftovers. 12 to 15 servings.

* HOT FUDGE VARIATION: (Since the Hot Fudge flavor of CHOCOLATE SHOPPE TOPPING is thicker than the other varieties, follow these directions.) Prepare crumb-butter bottom as directed above. Place open jar HERSHEY'S Hot Fudge Chocolate Shoppe Topping in microwave oven; heat as directed on label. Carefully spread warm fudge topping on top of crumb-butter mixture in pan; prepare, freeze, serve and store dessert as directed above.

THREE-IN-ONE CHOCOLATE PUDDING & PIE FILLING

¾ cup sugar
⅓ cup HERSHEY'S Cocoa
2 tablespoons cornstarch
2 tablespoons all-purpose flour
¼ teaspoon salt

2 cups milk
2 eggs, slightly beaten
2 tablespoons butter or margarine
1 teaspoon vanilla extract

In medium saucepan, stir together sugar, cocoa, cornstarch, flour and salt; blend in milk and eggs. Cook over medium heat, stirring constantly, until mixture boils; boil and stir 1 minute. Remove from heat; blend in butter and vanilla. Pour into individual serving dishes; press plastic wrap directly onto surface. Cool; refrigerate. 4 servings.

PARFAITS: Alternate layers of cold pudding and sweetened whipped cream or whipped topping in parfait glasses.

PIE: Reduce milk to 1¾ cups in recipe above; cook as directed. Stir in butter and vanilla. Pour hot pudding into 8-inch (6 oz.) packaged crumb crust; press plastic wrap onto surface. Refrigerate; top with sweetened whipped cream or whipped topping before serving. 6 servings.

Microwave Directions: In 2-quart microwave-safe bowl, combine sugar, cocoa, cornstarch, flour and salt; blend in milk and egg yolks. Microwave at HIGH (100%) 5 minutes, stirring several times or until mixture boils. Microwave at HIGH 1 to 2 additional minutes or until mixture is smooth and thickened.

PEANUT BUTTER-CHOCOLATE RIPPLE POPS

1 package (4 serving size) vanilla
    pudding and pie filling mix*
2 cups milk
1 cup REESE'S Peanut Butter Chips
1/2 cup HERSHEY'S MINI CHIPS
    Semi-Sweet Chocolate or
    HERSHEY'S Semi-Sweet
    Chocolate Chips

1 envelope (1.3 oz.) dry whipped
    topping mix
1/2 cup cold milk
1/2 teaspoon vanilla extract
10 paper cups (3-oz. size)
10 wooden popsicle sticks

Cook pudding as directed on package, using 2 cups milk. In small bowl, measure 1 cup hot cooked pudding. Immediately add peanut butter chips; stir until chips are melted and mixture is smooth. Add chocolate chips to remaining hot pudding in saucepan; stir until chips are melted and mixture is smooth. Press plastic wrap directly onto surface of each mixture; refrigerate 30 minutes. Prepare whipped topping mix as directed on package, using 1/2 cup cold milk and vanilla. Add half of whipped topping to peanut butter mixture and half to chocolate mixture; blend each well. Spoon about 1 tablespoon peanut butter mixture into each paper cup; top with 1 tablespoon chocolate mixture. Repeat layers. Insert popsicle stick into center; freeze 4 hours or until firm. Peel off paper cups to serve. 10 pops.

*Do not use instant pudding mix.

HERSHEY BAR MOUSSE

1 HERSHEY'S Milk Chocolate Bar (7
    oz.), broken into pieces
1/4 cup water

2 eggs, slightly beaten
1 cup (1/2 pt.) cold whipping cream

Line 8-inch square pan with foil. In medium microwave-safe bowl, place chocolate and water. Microwave at HIGH (100%) 1 1/2 minutes or until chocolate is softened. Stir until chocolate is melted and mixture is smooth. (If necessary, microwave at HIGH a few additional seconds to melt chocolate). Stir in beaten eggs. Microwave at MEDIUM (50%) 1 1/2 to 2 1/2 minutes or until mixture is very hot, but not boiling. Cool to lukewarm. In small mixer bowl, beat whipping cream until stiff; fold into chocolate mixture. Pour into prepared pan. Cover; freeze until firm. Cut into squares; serve frozen. About 4 servings.

CONVENTIONAL DIRECTIONS: In top of double boiler over hot, not boiling water, place chocolate bar pieces and 1/4 cup water; stir constantly until chocolate is melted and mixture is smooth. Add eggs; cook and stir over hot water about 2 minutes. Remove from heat; cool to room temperature. In small mixer bowl, beat whipping cream until stiff; fold in cooled chocolate mixture. Spoon into prepared pan as directed above.

DOUBLE CHOCOLATE DIPPING SAUCE

1 cup sugar
1 can (5 oz.) evaporated milk
1/2 cup light corn syrup
1/2 cup HERSHEY'S Cocoa
1/4 cup water

1/4 cup (1/2 stick) butter or margarine
1 HERSHEY'S Milk Chocolate Bar (7
    oz.), broken into pieces
1 teaspoon vanilla extract
Fruit pieces or small pieces of cake

In heavy medium saucepan, stir together sugar, evaporated milk, corn syrup, cocoa, water and butter. Over medium heat, stirring constantly, heat to boiling; boil and stir 3 minutes. Remove from heat. Stir in chocolate and vanilla, stirring until completely blended. If necessary, return saucepan to heat to finish melting chocolate. Cool slightly. May be served warm or at room temperature with fruit pieces or cake pieces. About 2 1/2 cups sauce.

TWO GREAT TASTES PUDDING PARFAITS

1 package (6 serving size) vanilla
   pudding and pie filling
3½ cups milk
1 cup REESE'S Peanut Butter Chips

1 cup HERSHEY'S Semi-Sweet
   Chocolate Chips or Semi-Sweet
   Chocolate Chunks
Whipped topping (optional)

In large heavy saucepan, combine pudding mix and 3½ cups milk (rather than amount listed in package directions). Cook over medium heat, stirring constantly, until mixture comes to full boil. Remove from heat; divide hot mixture between 2 heatproof medium bowls. Immediately stir peanut butter chips into mixture in one bowl and chocolate chips into mixture in second bowl. Stir both mixtures until chips are melted and mixture is smooth. Cool slightly, stirring occasionally. In parfait glasses, wine glasses or dessert dishes, alternately layer peanut butter and chocolate mixtures. Place plastic wrap directly onto surface of each dessert; refrigerate several hours or overnight. Garnish with whipped topping, if desired. About 4 to 6 servings.

CHOCOLATE-MARSHMALLOW MOUSSE

1 HERSHEY'S Milk Chocolate Bar (7
   oz.), broken into pieces
1½ cups miniature marshmallows

⅓ cup milk
1 cup (½ pt.) cold whipping cream

In medium microwave-safe bowl, place chocolate with marshmallows and milk. Microwave at HIGH (100%) 1 to 1½ minutes or just until mixture is smooth when stirred; cool to room temperature. In small mixer bowl, beat whipping cream until stiff; fold into chocolate mixture. Pour into dessert dishes. Cover; refrigerate 1 to 2 hours or until set. 6 servings.

VARIATIONS:

CHOCOLATE-MARSHMALLOW MOUSSE PARFAITS: Prepare MOUSSE according to directions. Alternately spoon mousse and sweetened whipped cream or whipped topping into parfait glasses. Cover; refrigerate about 1 hour. 4 to 6 servings.

CHOCOLATE-MARSHMALLOW MOUSSE PIE: Prepare MOUSSE according to directions. Pour into 8-inch (6 oz.) packaged chocolate flavored crumb crust. Cover; refrigerate 2 to 3 hours or until firm. Garnish as desired. 8 servings.

CHOCOLATE BAVARIAN CREAM

1 tablespoon unflavored gelatin
¼ cup cold water
2 bars (2 oz.) HERSHEY'S
   Unsweetened Baking Chocolate
1 cup sugar
Dash salt

½ cup hot milk
1 teaspoon vanilla extract
1½ cups cold whipping cream
CHOCOLATE CRUST (recipe follows)
Sweetened whipped cream

In small cup, sprinkle gelatin onto cold water; let stand a few minutes to soften. In medium microwave-safe bowl, place chocolate. Microwave at HIGH (100%) 1 minute or until chocolate is melted and smooth when stirred. Add sugar, salt and hot milk; blend well. Stir in gelatin mixture. Cool to lukewarm; beat mixture 2 minutes or until lightly thickened. Add vanilla. In small mixer bowl, beat whipping cream until stiff; fold into chocolate mixture. Pour filling over prepared crust; refrigerate until set. Cut into squares. Garnish with sweetened whipped cream. Refrigerate leftovers. 12 servings.

CHOCOLATE CRUST: Heat oven to 350°F. In 9-inch square pan, stir together 1 cup vanilla wafer crumbs (about 30 wafers), ¼ cup HERSHEY'S Cocoa and ¼ cup powdered sugar. Stir in ¼ cup melted butter or margarine; blend well. Press evenly onto bottom of pan. Bake 10 minutes. Cool completely.

CHOCOLATE PEANUT BUTTER SPREAD

1 cup HERSHEY'S Syrup

1 cup REESE'S Creamy or Crunchy Peanut Butter

In small bowl, combine syrup and peanut butter. Use as a spread on crackers, rice cakes, bread, etc. About 1¾ cups spread.

CHOCOLATE MOUSSE & RASPBERRIES

4 bars (4 oz.) HERSHEY'S Unsweetened Baking Chocolate, broken into pieces
1 can (14 oz.) sweetened condensed milk

2 teaspoons vanilla extract
2 cups (1 pt.) cold whipping cream
RASPBERRY TOPPING (recipe follows)

In heavy saucepan over medium-low heat, melt chocolate with sweetened condensed milk; stir in vanilla. Pour into large bowl; cool to room temperature, about 1½ hours. Beat until smooth. In large mixer bowl, beat whipping cream until stiff; fold into chocolate mixture. Spoon mousse into dessert dishes. Refrigerate until thoroughly chilled. Serve with RASPBERRY TOPPING. Refrigerate leftovers. 8 servings.

RASPBERRY TOPPING: Drain 1 package (10 oz.) thawed frozen red raspberries, reserving syrup. In small saucepan, stir together ⅔ cup reserved syrup, ¼ cup red currant jelly or red raspberry jam and 1 tablespoon cornstarch. Cook over low heat, stirring constantly, until thickened and clear. Cool. Stir in raspberries. About 1⅓ cups sauce.

CHOCOLATE PEANUT BUTTER SAUCE

½ cup HERSHEY'S CHOCOLATE SHOPPE HOT FUDGE Topping or HERSHEY'S Chocolate Fudge Topping

½ cup HERSHEY'S Syrup
¼ cup REESE'S Creamy Peanut Butter

In small saucepan, Place all ingredients. Cook over low heat, stirring constantly, until mixture is warm. Serve immediately over ice cream or other desserts. About 1¼ cups sauce.

To reheat: Place sauce in small saucepan. Stir constantly over low heat until warm.

BLACK FOREST FONDUE

Two jars (12 oz. each) maraschino cherries with stems
1 HERSHEY'S Milk Chocolate Bar (7 oz.), broken into pieces

1 HERSHEY'S SPECIAL DARK Bar (7 oz.), broken into pieces
½ cup light cream
2 to 3 tablespoons kirsch (cherry brandy) (optional)

Drain cherries; set aside. (Cherries may be placed on flat tray in freezer for at least one hour before serving, if desired). Place chocolate in medium saucepan with light cream. Cook over very low heat, stirring constantly, until chocolate is melted and mixture is smooth. Remove from heat; add liqueur. If mixture thickens, stir in additional light cream, one tablespoon at a time. Pour into fondue pot; dip cherries into warm fondue. About 2 cups fondue.

CANDIES AND SNACKS

RAGTIME ROCKY ROAD

2 HERSHEY'S Milk Chocolate Bars
  (7 oz. each), broken into pieces
3 cups miniature marshmallows

¾ cup coarsely broken walnuts or
  pecans

Butter 8-inch square pan. In top of double boiler, over hot, not boiling, water, melt chocolate bar pieces; stir in marshmallows and walnuts. Spread mixture into prepared pan. Refrigerate until firm. Cut into squares. 16 squares.

S'MORES CANDY

¾ cup light corn syrup
3 tablespoons butter or margarine
2 cups (11.5-oz. pkg.) HERSHEY'S
  Milk Chocolate Chips

8 cups honey graham cereal
3 cups miniature marshmallows

Grease 13x9x2-inch pan. In medium saucepan over low heat, stirring constantly, cook corn syrup, butter and chocolate chips until chips are melted and mixture boils. Remove from heat; pour over cereal in large mixing bowl. Toss until cereal is completely coated; stir in marshmallows, 1 cup at a time. Press mixture evenly into prepared pan. Let stand until firm, about 1 hour. Store covered at room temperature. Cut into squares. About 2 dozen squares.

CHERRIES 'N CHOCOLATE FUDGE

1 can (14 oz.) sweetened condensed
  milk
2 cups (12-oz.pkg.) HERSHEY'S
  Semi-Sweet Chocolate Chips

½ cup coarsely chopped almonds
½ cup chopped candied cherries
1 teaspoon almond extract

Line 8-inch square pan with foil. In medium microwave-safe bowl, combine sweetened condensed milk and chocolate chips; stir lightly. Microwave at HIGH (100%) 1½ to 2 minutes or until chips are melted and mixture is smooth when stirred. Stir in almonds, cherries and almond extract. Spread evenly in prepared pan. Cover; refrigerate until firm. Cut into 1-inch squares. Cover; store in refrigerator. About 4 dozen squares.

MERRY CHOCOLATE NUT CLUSTERS

1 cup HERSHEY'S Semi-Sweet
  Chocolate Chips
½ cup HERSHEY'S Vanilla Milk
  Chips

1 tablespoon shortening
2¼ cups (11.5 oz.) lightly salted
  peanuts, divided

In small microwave-safe bowl, place chocolate chips, vanilla milk chips and shortening. Microwave at HIGH (100%) 1 to 1½ minutes or until chips are melted and mixture is smooth when stirred. Reserve ¼ cup peanuts for garnish; stir remaining peanuts into chocolate mixture. Drop by teaspoonfuls into 1-inch diameter candy papers; top each candy with peanut. Refrigerate, uncovered, until chocolate is set, about 1 hour. Store in airtight container in cool, dry place. About 3 dozen candies.

HERSHEY'S VANILLA MILK CHIPS ALMOND FUDGE

1²/₃ cups (10-oz. pkg.) HERSHEY'S
   Vanilla Milk Chips
²/₃ cup sweetened condensed milk

1¹/₂ cups coarsely chopped slivered
   almonds, toasted*
¹/₂ teaspoon vanilla extract

Butter 8-inch square pan. In medium saucepan over very low heat, melt vanilla milk chips and sweetened condensed milk, stirring constantly, until mixture is smooth. Remove from heat. Stir in almonds and vanilla. Spread in prepared pan. Cover; refrigerate until firm, about 2 hours. Cut into 1-inch squares. About 4 dozen candies.

* To toast almonds: Spread almonds on cookie sheet. Bake at 350°F., stirring occasionally, 8 to 10 minutes or until lightly browned; cool.

CHOCOLATE PEANUT BUTTER CHIP FUDGE

2 cups (12-oz. pkg.) HERSHEY'S
   Semi-Sweet Chocolate Chips
1 can (14 oz.) sweetened condensed
   milk

1 teaspoon vanilla extract
Dash salt
1 cup REESE'S Peanut Butter Chips

Line 8-inch square pan with foil; set aside. In heavy saucepan over low heat, stir chocolate chips, sweetened condensed milk, vanilla and salt until chips are melted and mixture is smooth. Remove from heat. Add peanut butter chips; stir just to distribute chips throughout mixture. Spread evenly into prepared pan. Refrigerate 2 hours or until firm. Remove from pan; peel off foil. Cut into squares. Store tightly covered in refrigerator. 3 dozen pieces or about 2 pounds.

CHOCO-PEANUT BUTTER DROPS

2 cups (12-oz. pkg.) HERSHEY'S
   Semi-Sweet Chocolate Chips
1 can (14-oz.) sweetened condensed
   milk
1 cup miniature marshmallows

1 cup coarsely chopped peanuts
²/₃ cup REESE'S Creamy Peanut
   Butter
2 teaspoons vanilla extract

In medium saucepan over low heat, combine chocolate chips, sweetened condensed milk and marshmallows. Heat, stirring constantly until marshmallows are melted and mixture is smooth. Remove from heat; stir in chopped peanuts, peanut butter and vanilla. Spoon rounded teaspoonfuls into 1-inch paper candy cups or paper-lined mini muffin cups. Cover; refrigerate at least 15 minutes before serving. Refrigerate leftovers. About 72 candies.

Note: Recipe may be halved.

PEANUT BUTTER MELTAWAY FUDGE

3¹/₂ cups sugar
1¹/₂ cups (12-oz. can) evaporated milk
¹/₂ cup (1 stick) butter or margarine
2 tablespoons light corn syrup

1 tablespoon white vinegar
2¹/₂ cups REESE'S Creamy or
   Crunchy Peanut Butter
1 jar (7 oz.) marshmallow creme

In 4-quart saucepan, combine sugar, evaporated milk, butter, corn syrup, and vinegar. Cook over medium heat, stirring constantly, until mixture comes to full rolling boil; boil and stir 5 minutes. Remove from heat. Add peanut butter and marshmallow creme; stir until smooth. Pour into ungreased 13x9x2-inch pan. Cool; cut into squares. About 8 dozen squares or about 4 pounds candy.

CHOCOLATE PEANUT BUTTER FUDGE

4 cups sugar
1 jar (7 oz.) marshmallow creme
1½ cups (12-oz. can) evaporated milk
1 cup REESE'S Creamy or Crunchy
   Peanut Butter

1 tablespoon butter or margarine
1 cup HERSHEY'S Semi-Sweet
   Chocolate Chips

Line 13x9x2-inch pan with foil, extending foil over edges of pan. Butter foil lightly; set aside. In heavy 4-quart saucepan, stir together sugar, marshmallow creme, evaporated milk, peanut butter and butter. Cook over medium heat, stirring constantly, until mixture comes to full rolling boil; boil and stir 5 minutes. Remove from heat; immediately add chocolate chips, stirring until smooth. Pour into prepared pan; cool until firm. Use foil to lift fudge out of pan; peel off foil. Cut into squares. Store tightly covered in a cool, dry place. About 8 dozen squares or 3½ pounds candy.

CHOCOLATE-ALMOND FUDGE

4 cups sugar
1 jar (7 oz.) marshmallow creme
1½ cups (12-oz. can) evaporated milk
1 tablespoon butter or margarine
2 cups (12-oz. pkg.) HERSHEY'S
   Semi-Sweet Chocolate Chips

1 HERSHEY'S Milk Chocolate Bar (7
   oz.), broken into pieces
1 teaspoon vanilla extract
¾ cup slivered almonds, toasted and
   coarsely chopped*

Line 9-inch square pan with foil; set aside. In heavy 4-quart saucepan, stir together sugar, marshmallow creme, evaporated milk and butter. Cook over medium heat, stirring constantly, until mixture comes to full rolling boil; boil, stirring constantly 7 minutes. Remove from heat; immediately add chocolate chips and chocolate bar pieces, stirring until chocolate is melted and mixture is smooth. Stir in vanilla and almonds. Pour into prepared pan; cool until firm. Cut into 1-inch squares. Store in tightly covered container. About 5 dozen squares or about 4 pounds.

* To toast almonds: Heat oven to 350°F. Spread almonds in thin layer in shallow baking pan. Bake 8 to 10 minutes, stirring occasionally, until light golden brown; cool.

VARIATION: 1 HERSHEY'S Milk Chocolate Bar With Almonds (7-oz.) may be substituted for HERSHEY'S Milk Chocolate Bar.

SPECIAL DARK TRUFFLES

1 HERSHEY'S SPECIAL DARK
   Chocolate Bar (7 oz.), broken into
   pieces
½ cup whipping cream

¼ cup finely chopped pecans
¼ cup powdered sugar
2 tablespoons HERSHEY'S Cocoa

Butter 8- or 9-inch pan. In small saucepan, stir together chocolate pieces, whipping cream and pecans. Cook over low heat, stirring constantly, until chocolate is melted and mixture is well blended. Pour into prepared pan; refrigerate 2 hours or until firm. In small bowl, stir together powdered sugar and cocoa. To prepare truffles, with hands, roll small spoonfuls of mixture into ¾-inch balls. (If mixture becomes too soft, return to refrigerator until firm.) Gently roll balls in cocoa mixture, coating all sides. Store in refrigerator. Reroll truffles in cocoa mixture before serving, if desired. About 2½ dozen truffles.

CREAMY DOUBLE DECKER FUDGE

1 cup REESE'S Peanut Butter Chips
1 can (14 oz.) sweetened condensed
  milk, divided

1 teaspoon vanilla extract, divided
1 cup HERSHEY'S Semi-Sweet
  Chocolate Chips

Line 8-inch square pan with foil; set aside. In small microwave-safe bowl, place peanut butter chips and ⅔ cup sweetened condensed milk. Microwave at HIGH (100%) 1 to 1½ minutes, stirring after 1 minute, until chips are melted and mixture is smooth when stirred. Stir in ½ teaspoon vanilla; spread evenly into prepared pan. In small microwave-safe bowl, place remaining sweetened condensed milk and chocolate chips; repeat above microwave procedure. Stir in remaining ½ teaspoon vanilla; spread evenly over peanut butter layer. Cover; refrigerate until firm. Cut into 1-inch squares. Store in tightly covered container in refrigerator. About 4 dozen squares or 1½ pounds.

RICH COCOA FUDGE

3 cups sugar
⅔ cup HERSHEY'S Cocoa or
  HERSHEY'S European Style
  Cocoa

⅛ teaspoon salt
1½ cups milk
¼ cup (½ stick) butter or margarine
1 teaspoon vanilla extract

Line 8-or 9-inch square pan with foil; butter foil. Set aside. In heavy 4-quart saucepan, stir together sugar, cocoa and salt; stir in milk. Cook over medium heat, stirring constantly, until mixture comes to full rolling boil. Boil, without stirring, to 234°F or until syrup, when dropped into very cold water, forms a soft ball which flattens when removed from water. (Bulb of candy thermometer should not rest on bottom of saucepan). Remove from heat. Add butter and vanilla. DO NOT STIR. Cool at room temperature to 110°F (lukewarm). Beat with wooden spoon until fudge thickens and loses some of its gloss. Quickly spread into prepared pan; cool. Cut into squares. About 36 pieces or 1¾ pounds.

VARIATIONS:
NUTTY RICH COCOA FUDGE: Beat cooked fudge as directed. Immediately stir in 1 cup chopped almonds, pecans or walnuts and quickly spread into prepared pan.

MARSHMALLOW-NUT COCOA FUDGE: Increase cocoa to ¾ cup. Cook fudge as directed. Add 1 cup marshmallow creme with butter and vanilla. DO NOT STIR. Cool to 110°F (lukewarm). Beat 10 minutes; stir in 1 cup chopped nuts and pour into prepared pan. (Fudge does not set until poured into pan.)

CRISPY PEPPERMINT MARSHMALLOW TREATS

¼ cup (½ stick) butter or margarine
15 small (1½ inch) YORK Peppermint
  Patties, unwrapped and quartered

4 cups miniature marshmallows
5 cups crisp rice cereal

Grease 9-inch square pan. In large bowl, place butter and quartered patties. Microwave at HIGH (100%) 1 minute or until melted and smooth when stirred. Add marshmallows; toss to coat with butter mixture. Microwave at HIGH 45 seconds or until smooth when stirred. Immediately add cereal; stir until well coated. Press into prepared pan. Cool; cut into squares. About 24 squares.

BUTTER ALMOND CRUNCH

1½ cups HERSHEY'S MINI CHIPS
    Semi-Sweet Chocolate or
    HERSHEY'S Semi-Sweet
    Chocolate Chips, divided
1¾ cups chopped almonds, divided

1½ cups (3 sticks) butter or margarine
1¾ cups sugar
3 tablespoons light corn syrup
3 tablespoons water

Heat oven to 350°F. Line 13x9x2-inch pan with foil; butter foil. Sprinkle 1 cup chocolate chips into pan; set aside. In shallow baking pan, spread almonds. Bake 7 minutes or until golden brown; set aside. In heavy 3-quart saucepan, melt butter; blend in sugar, corn syrup and water. Cook over medium heat, stirring constantly, to 300°F. on a candy thermometer or until syrup, when dropped into very cold water, separates into threads which are hard and brittle. Remove from heat; stir in 1½ cups toasted almonds. Immediately spread mixture evenly over chocolate chips in prepared pan; do not disturb chips. Sprinkle with remaining ¼ cup toasted almonds and remaining ½ cup chocolate chips; cool slightly. With sharp knife, score into 1½-inch squares, wiping knife blade after drawing through candy. Cool completely; remove from pan. Remove foil; break into pieces. Store in tightly covered container in cool, dry place. About 2 pounds candy.

CHOCOLATE & VANILLA HEARTS

1 cup HERSHEY'S Semi-Sweet
    Chocolate Chips or HERSHEY'S
    Milk Chocolate Chips
2 tablespoons shortening, divided (not
    butter, margarine or oil)

¾ cup HERSHEY'S Vanilla Milk
    Chips
¼ cup finely ground nuts

In small microwave-safe bowl, place chocolate chips and 1 tablespoon shortening. Microwave at HIGH (100%) 1 minute; stir. If necessary, microwave at HIGH an additional 30 seconds or until chocolate is melted and smooth when stirred. Spoon into heart-shaped ice cube tray or candy molds, filling each ½ full; tap molds to release air bubbles and smooth surface. Refrigerate 8 to 10 minutes to partially set chocolate. Meanwhile, in small microwave-safe bowl, place vanilla milk chips and 1 tablespoon shortening. Microwave at HIGH 1 minute; stir. If necessary, microwave at HIGH an additional 30 seconds or until melted and smooth when stirred; stir in nuts. Spoon onto chocolate layer; tap to smooth surface. Refrigerate several hours or until firm. Invert tray or molds and tap lightly to release heart candies. About 10 candies.

VARIATIONS:

ALMOND: Add 2 or 3 drops almond extract to melted chocolate chips.

CHERRY: Omit nuts; add ¼ cup finely chopped red candied cherries and 2 or 3 drops red food color to melted vanilla chips.

MINT: Add ¼ teaspoon mint extract and 2 or 3 drops red or green food color to vanilla milk chips.

CHEWY COCOA AND PEANUT BUTTER TREATS

1 cup light corn syrup
1 cup packed light brown sugar
1⅔ cups (10-oz.pkg.) REESE'S Peanut
    Butter Chips

¼ cup HERSHEY'S Cocoa
2 tablespoons butter or margarine
6 cups crisp rice cereal

Butter 13x9x2-inch pan. In large saucepan, stir together corn syrup and brown sugar. Cook over medium heat, stirring constantly, until mixture comes to a boil. Remove from heat. Add peanut butter chips, cocoa and butter; stir until chips are melted and mixture is smooth. (Mixture will be thick.) Add cereal; stir until well coated. Immediately press into prepared pan. Cool thoroughly. Cut into squares. About 30 treats.

COCOA OATMEAL TREATS

2 cups sugar
1/3 cup HERSHEY'S Cocoa
1/2 cup milk
1/2 cup (1 stick) butter or margarine

1/3 cup REESE'S Creamy or Crunchy
  Peanut Butter
2 1/2 cups quick-cooking rolled oats
1/2 cup chopped unsalted peanuts

In medium saucepan, stir together sugar and cocoa; stir in milk and butter. Cook over medium heat, stirring constantly, until mixture comes to a boil; boil 1 minute. Remove from heat; stir in peanut butter. Add oats and peanuts; stir to mix well. Quickly drop mixture by rounded teaspoonfuls onto wax paper or foil. Cool completely. Store in cool, dry place. About 4 dozen.

INDOOR S'MORES

6 graham crackers, broken into halves
1 HERSHEY'S Milk Chocolate Bar
  (1.55 oz.), broken into pieces

3 marshmallows, cut into halves

Place 1 graham cracker half on paper towel; center 1 marshmallow half on cracker. Microwave at HIGH (100%) 10 to 15 seconds or just until marshmallow begins to puff. Immediately top with 2 pieces milk chocolate bar and graham cracker half; press together gently. Repeat for each serving. Serve immediately. 6 servings.

MUDDY BUDDIES

9 cups favorite bite-size crisp corn,
  rice or wheat cereal
1 cup HERSHEY'S Semi-Sweet
  Chocolate Chips

1/2 cup REESE'S Peanut Butter
1/4 cup (1/2 stick) butter or margarine
1/4 teaspoon vanilla extract
1 1/2 cups powdered sugar

In large bowl, place cereal. In medium microwave-safe bowl, place chocolate chips, peanut butter and butter. Microwave at HIGH (100%) 1 1/2 minutes or until mixture is smooth when stirred. Stir in vanilla. Pour chocolate mixture over cereal, stirring until all pieces are evenly coated. Pour mixture into large plastic bag with powdered sugar; shake until all pieces are coated. Spread on wax paper to cool. Store leftovers in air-tight container. About 9 cups.

COCOA CRISPY TREATS

6 tablespoons butter or margarine
1/4 cup REESE'S Creamy Peanut
  Butter
1 package (10 oz., about 40) regular
  marshmallows, OR 4 cups
  miniature marshmallows

1/3 cup HERSHEY'S Cocoa
4 cups crisp rice cereal
1/2 cup unsalted peanuts, raisins, nuts,
  REESE'S Peanut Butter Chips or
  HERSHEY'S Semi-Sweet
  Chocolate Chips

Butter 9-inch square baking pan. In large saucepan, over low heat, melt butter and peanut butter. Add marshmallows; stir until completely melted and well blended. Remove from heat. Stir in cocoa; blend well. Add crisp rice cereal and peanuts; stir until cereal is well coated. Using buttered spatula or wax paper, press mixture evenly into prepared pan. Cool completely; cut into squares. About 16 squares.

CHOCOLATE DIPPED SNACKS

½ cup HERSHEY'S Milk Chocolate
   Chips
½ cup HERSHEY'S Semi-Sweet
   Chocolate Chips

1 tablespoon shortening (not butter,
   margarine or oil)
Potato chips, cookies, dried apricots
   or miniature pretzels

Cover tray with wax paper. In small microwave-safe bowl, place chocolate chips and shortening. Microwave at HIGH (100%) 1 to 1½ minutes or just until chips are melted and mixture is smooth when stirred; cool slightly. Dip ⅔ of each snack or fruit into chocolate mixture. Shake gently to remove excess chocolate. Place on prepared tray. Refrigerate, uncovered, about 30 minutes or until coating is firm. Store in airtight container in cool, dry place. About ½ cup coating.

CHOCOLATE SNACK BLOCKS

3 envelopes unflavored gelatin
¾ cup cold water
1 cup boiling water
⅓ cup sugar

2 cups (12-oz. pkg.) HERSHEY'S
   MINI CHIPS Semi-Sweet
   Chocolate

In blender, sprinkle gelatin over cold water; let stand 5 minutes. Add boiling water and sugar; cover, blending on low speed until gelatin is completely dissolved, about 2 minutes. Continue to blend, gradually adding small chocolate chips, until chips are melted and mixture is smooth. Pour into 8-or 9-inch square pan. Refrigerate until firm. Cut into 1-inch squares or shapes with cookie cutters. About 6 dozen squares.

VANILLA COVERED STRAWBERRIES

1⅔ cups (10-oz. pkg.) HERSHEY'S
   Vanilla Milk Chips
1 tablespoon butter flavor shortening

Fresh strawberries, rinsed and patted
   dry

Cover tray with wax paper. In medium microwave-safe bowl, place vanilla milk chips and shortening. Microwave at HIGH (100%) 30 seconds; stir. Microwave additional 15 seconds at a time until smooth when stirred vigorously. Holding by top, dip ⅔ of each strawberry into vanilla mixture; shake gently to remove excess. Place on prepared tray. Refrigerate until coating is firm. Store, covered, in refrigerator. Coats about 4 dozen small strawberries. (About ¾ cup coating.)

CHOCOLATE COVERED STRAWBERRIES

2 cups (12-oz. pkg.) HERSHEY'S
   Semi-Sweet Chocolate Chips
2 tablespoons shortening (not butter,
   margarine or oil*)

Fresh strawberries with stems, rinsed
   and patted dry

Cover tray with wax paper. In medium microwave-safe bowl, place chocolate chips and shortening. Microwave at HIGH (100%) 1½ minutes or just until chips are melted and mixture is smooth when stirred; cool slightly. Holding by top, dip ⅔ of each strawberry into chocolate mixture; shake gently to remove excess. Place on prepared tray. Refrigerate until coating is firm, about 30 minutes. Store, covered, in refrigerator. Coats about 5 dozen small strawberries. (About 1 cup coating)

* Butter and margarine contain water which may prevent chocolate from melting properly and oil may prevent chocolate from forming a coating.

COOKIES

OATMEAL BROWNIE DROPS

½ cup (½ stick) butter or margarine,
   softened
¾ cup sugar
2 eggs
1 teaspoon vanilla extract
1 cup all-purpose flour

½ cup HERSHEY'S Cocoa
¼ teaspoon baking soda
1 cup quick-cooking rolled oats
1 cup HERSHEY'S MINI CHIPS
   Semi-Sweet Chocolate

Heat oven to 350°F. In large mixer bowl, beat together butter and sugar until well blended. Add eggs and vanilla; blend thoroughly. Stir together flour, cocoa and baking soda; add to butter mixture, blending thoroughly. Stir in oats and small chocolate chips. Drop by tablespoonfuls onto ungreased cookie sheet. Bake 7 to 8 minutes or until cookie begins to set. Do not overbake. Remove from cookie sheet to wire rack. Cool completely. About 3½ dozen cookies.

PEANUT BUTTER OATMEAL RAISIN DROPS

1 cup (2 sticks) butter or margarine,
   softened
1 cup packed light brown sugar
½ cup granulated sugar
1 cup REESE'S Creamy or Crunchy
   Peanut Butter
2 eggs

1 teaspoon vanilla extract
1½ cups all-purpose flour
1 teaspoon baking soda
½ teaspoon salt
2 cups quick-cooking or regular rolled
   oats
1 cup raisins

Heat oven to 375°F. In large mixer bowl, beat butter, brown sugar and granulated sugar until well blended. Add peanut butter, eggs and vanilla; blend well. Stir together flour, baking soda and salt. Add to butter mixture; blend well. Stir in oats and raisins. Drop by rounded teaspoonfuls onto ungreased cookie sheet. Bake 8 to 10 minutes or until lightly browned. Cool slightly; remove from cookie sheet to wire rack. Cool completely. About 5 dozen cookies.

CHOCOLATE OATMEAL WALNUT COOKIES

4 bars (4 oz.) HERSHEY'S
   Unsweetened Baking Chocolate,
   broken into pieces
¾ cup (1½ sticks) butter or
   margarine, softened
2 cups sugar
2 eggs
1 teaspoon vanilla extract
2 cups all-purpose flour

1 teaspoon baking soda
1 teaspoon ground cinnamon
   (optional)
½ teaspoon salt
½ cup milk
3 cups regular or quick-cooking rolled
   oats
1½ cups coarsely chopped walnuts

Heat oven to 350°F. Lightly grease cookie sheet. In small microwave-safe bowl, place chocolate. Microwave at HIGH (100%) 1 to 1½ minutes or until chocolate is melted when stirred; cool slightly. In large mixer bowl, beat butter and sugar until well blended. Add eggs; blend well. Blend in vanilla and melted chocolate. Add flour, baking soda, cinnamon, if desired, and salt; blend just until moistened. Gradually add milk, blending well. Stir in oats and walnuts. Drop by tablespoonfuls onto prepared cookie sheet. Bake 10 to 11 minutes or just until set. Cool 1 minute; remove from cookie sheet to wire rack. Cool completely. About 5 dozen cookies.

JOLLY PEANUT BUTTER GINGERBREAD COOKIES

1²/₃ cups (10-oz. pkg.) REESE'S
   Peanut Butter Chips
³/₄ cup (1½ sticks) butter or
   margarine, softened
1 cup packed light brown sugar
1 cup dark corn syrup

2 eggs
5 cups all-purpose flour
1 teaspoon baking soda
½ teaspoon ground cinnamon
¼ teaspoon ground ginger
¼ teaspoon salt

In small microwave-safe bowl, place peanut butter chips. Microwave at HIGH (100%) 1 to 2 minutes or until chips are melted when stirred. In large mixer bowl, beat melted peanut butter chips and butter until well blended. Add brown sugar, corn syrup and eggs; beat until light and fluffy. Stir together flour, baking soda, cinnamon, ginger and salt. Add half of flour mixture to butter mixture; beat on low speed of electric mixer until smooth. With wooden spoon, stir in remaining flour mixture until well blended. Divide into thirds; wrap each in plastic wrap. Refrigerate until dough is firm enough to roll, at least 1 hour. Heat oven to 325°F. On lightly floured surface, roll 1 dough portion at a time to ⅛-inch thickness; with floured cookie cutters, cut into holiday shapes. Place on ungreased cookie sheet. Bake 10 to 12 minutes or until set and lightly browned. Cool slightly; remove from cookie sheet to wire rack. Cool completely. Frost and decorate as desired. About 6 dozen cookies.

HALLOWEEN THUMBPRINT COOKIES

1 cup (2 sticks) butter or margarine,
   softened
1¹/₃ cups sugar
2 eggs
¼ cup milk
2 teaspoons vanilla extract

2 cups all-purpose flour
²/₃ cup HERSHEY'S Cocoa
½ teaspoon salt
ORANGE FILLING (recipe follows)
1 HERSHEY'S Milk Chocolate Bar (7
   oz.), cut into pieces

In large mixer bowl, beat butter, sugar, eggs, milk and vanilla until well blended. Stir together flour, cocoa and salt; add to butter mixture, mixing until well blended. Refrigerate dough 1 to 2 hours or until firm enough to handle. Heat oven to 350°F. Shape dough into 1-inch balls. Place on lightly greased cookie sheet. Press thumb gently in center of each cookie. (You may need to coat thumb with sugar for indentation to remain.) Bake 10 to 12 minutes or until set. Cool slightly; remove from cookie sheet to wire rack. Cool completely. Spoon about ¼ teaspoon ORANGE FILLING in each thumbprint. Gently press chocolate bar piece in center of each cookie. About 4 dozen cookies.

ORANGE FILLING: In small mixer bowl, combine 1 cup powdered sugar, 2 tablespoons softened butter or margarine, 4 teaspoons milk, ½ teaspoon freshly grated orange peel and ½ teaspoon vanilla extract; beat on high speed of electric mixer until smooth. Blend in yellow and red food color for desired orange color.

NO-BAKE PEANUT BUTTER CHIP COOKIES

1²/₃ cups (10-oz. pkg.) REESE'S
   Peanut Butter Chips
1 tablespoon shortening

5 cups corn flakes cereal
1 cup raisins

Cover tray with wax paper. In microwave-safe bowl, place peanut butter chips and shortening. Microwave at HIGH (100%) 1½ minutes or until smooth when stirred. Coarsely crush corn flakes; mix with melted peanut butter chips and raisins. Stir until cereal is coated. Drop by teaspoonfuls onto prepared tray. Cover; refrigerate one hour.

EASY PEANUT BLOSSOMS

1 can (14 oz.) sweetened condensed milk
¾ cup REESE'S Creamy Peanut Butter
2 cups all-purpose biscuit baking mix
1 teaspoon vanilla extract
Sugar
1 package (6 oz.) HERSHEY'S KISSES Chocolates, unwrapped

Heat oven to 375°F. In large mixer bowl, beat sweetened condensed milk and peanut butter until smooth. Add baking mix and vanilla; blend well. Shape into 1-inch balls; roll in sugar. Place 2 inches apart on ungreased cookie sheets. Bake 6 to 8 minutes or until very lightly browned (do not overbake). Remove from oven; immediately press unwrapped chocolate piece in center of each ball. Cool completely. Store in tightly covered container. About 3 dozen cookies.

PEANUT BUTTER CHIP PINEAPPLE DROPS

¼ cup (½ stick) butter or margarine, softened
¼ cup shortening
1 cup packed light brown sugar
1 egg
1 teaspoon vanilla extract
2 cups all-purpose flour
1 teaspoon baking powder
½ teaspoon baking soda
½ teaspoon salt
1 can (8 oz.) can crushed pineapple, drained
1 cup REESE'S Peanut Butter Chips
½ cup chopped nuts (optional)
Candied cherries, cut in half

Heat oven to 375°F. In large mixer bowl, beat butter and shortening until blended; add sugar, egg and vanilla. Beat until fluffy. Stir together flour, baking powder, baking soda and salt; add to butter mixture, blending well. Stir in pineapple, peanut butter chips and nuts. Drop by teaspoonfuls onto ungreased cookie sheet. Garnish with cherries. Bake 10 to 12 minutes or until lightly browned. Remove from cookie sheet to wire rack. Cool completely. About 3½ dozen.

PEANUT BUTTER COOKIES

¼ cup (½ stick) butter or margarine, softened
¼ cup shortening
½ cup REESE'S Creamy Peanut Butter
½ cup granulated sugar
½ cup packed light brown sugar
1 egg
1¼ cups all-purpose flour
¾ teaspoon baking soda
½ teaspoon baking powder
¼ teaspoon salt
¾ cup REESE'S Peanut Butter Chips
Granulated sugar

Heat oven to 375°F. In large mixer bowl, beat butter, shortening, peanut butter, ½ cup granulated sugar, brown sugar and egg. Blend in flour, baking soda, baking powder and salt; mix well. Stir in peanut butter chips. Shape into 1-inch balls; place on ungreased cookie sheet. With fork dipped in sugar, flatten in crisscross pattern. Bake 10 to 12 minutes or until set. Cool slightly; remove from cookie sheet to wire rack. Cool completely. About 4 dozen cookies.

PEPPERMINT PATTIE COOKIES

⅔ cup butter or margarine, softened
1 cup sugar
1 egg
½ teaspoon vanilla extract
1½ cups all-purpose flour
⅓ cup HERSHEY'S Cocoa

½ teaspoon baking soda
¼ teaspoon salt
1 tablespoon milk
12 to 14 small (1½-inch) YORK
  Peppermint Patties, unwrapped

In large mixer bowl, beat butter and sugar until creamy; add egg and vanilla, blending well. Stir together flour, cocoa, baking soda and salt. Add to butter mixture alternately with milk, blending well. Refrigerate dough about 1 hour or until firm enough to handle. (Dough will be a little soft.) Heat oven to 350°F. Lightly grease cookie sheet. Shape small portion of dough around peppermint pattie, completely covering candy. Place on prepared cookie sheet; flatten slightly and crimp with tines of fork around edge, if desired. Bake 10 to 12 minutes or until set. Cool 1 minute; remove from cookie sheet to wire rack. Cool completely. 12 to 14 cookies.

VANILLA CHIP APRICOT OATMEAL COOKIES

¾ cup (1½ sticks) butter or
  margarine, softened
½ cup granulated sugar
½ cup packed light brown sugar
1 egg
1 cup all-purpose flour

1 teaspoon baking soda
2½ cups rolled oats
1⅔ cups (10-oz. pkg.) HERSHEY'S
  Vanilla Milk Chips
½ cup chopped dried apricots

Heat oven to 375°F. In large mixer bowl, beat butter, granulated sugar and brown sugar until light and fluffy. Add egg; beat well. Blend in flour and baking soda. Stir in oats, vanilla milk chips and dried apricots. Drop by rounded teaspoonfuls onto ungreased cookie sheet. Bake 8 to 10 minutes or just until lightly browned; do not overbake. Cool slightly; remove from cookie sheet to wire rack. Cool completely. About 3½ dozen cookies.

PEANUT BUTTER CRISPS

1 cup (2 sticks) butter or margarine,
  softened and divided
1 cup sugar
¼ cup light corn syrup
1 egg
1 teaspoon vanilla extract

1⅔ cups (10-oz. pkg.) REESE'S
  Peanut Butter Chips
2 cups all-purpose flour
2 teaspoons baking soda
¼ teaspoon salt
Granulated sugar

In large mixer bowl, beat together ¾ cup (1½ sticks) butter and 1 cup sugar until light and fluffy. Add corn syrup, egg and vanilla; blend well. In medium microwave-safe bowl, place peanut butter chips and remaining ¼ cup butter. Microwave at HIGH (100%) 1 to 1½ minutes; stir until smooth when stirred. OR (Heat peanut butter chip mixture in saucepan over very low heat, stirring constantly, just until melted and smooth when stirred.) Blend into butter mixture. Stir together flour, baking soda and salt; add to peanut butter mixture, blending well. Refrigerate 1 hour or until firm enough to handle. Heat oven to 350°F. Shape dough into 1-inch balls; roll in sugar. Place on ungreased cookie sheet. Bake 10 to 12 minutes or until golden brown around edges. Cool slightly; remove from cookie sheet to wire rack. Cool completely. About 5 dozen cookies.

PEANUT BUTTER CRISSCROSSES

½ cup (1 stick) butter or margarine,
    softened
1 cup packed light brown sugar
¾ cup REESE'S Creamy or Crunchy
    Peanut Butter
1 egg

½ teaspoon vanilla extract
1¼ cups all-purpose flour
½ teaspoon baking powder
½ teaspoon baking soda
¼ teaspoon salt
Granulated sugar

In large mixer bowl, beat butter, brown sugar and peanut butter until well blended. Add egg and vanilla; beat well. Stir together flour, baking powder, baking soda and salt. Gradually add to peanut butter mixture; blending well. Refrigerate 1 hour or until firm enough to roll. Heat oven to 350°F. Lightly grease cookie sheet. Shape dough into 1½-inch balls; roll balls in granulated sugar. Place on prepared cookie sheet. With fork, flatten ball. Flatten again in opposite direction, forming crisscross marks. Bake 10 to 12 minutes or until light brown and cookie is set. Cool slightly; remove from cookie sheet to wire rack. Cool completely. About 3 dozen cookies.

PEANUTTY CHOCOLATE COOKIES

⅔ cup sugar
⅓ cup HERSHEY'S Cocoa
¼ teaspoon baking soda
½ cup milk

1⅔ cups (10-oz. pkg.) REESE'S
    Peanut Butter Chips
1 teaspoon vanilla extract
1 cup finely chopped peanuts
About 2½ dozen whole peanuts

In medium saucepan, combine sugar, cocoa and baking soda; blend in milk. Add peanut butter chips; stir over low heat until melted. Add vanilla; pour into medium bowl. Cool; refrigerate until set. Heat oven to 350°F. Roll spoonfuls of batter into 1-inch balls; roll balls in chopped peanuts. Flatten slightly; top with a whole peanut. Bake 8 to 10 minutes or until slightly firm, but not hard. Cool slightly; remove from cookie sheet to wire rack. Cool completely. About 2½ dozen cookies.

SECRET KISS COOKIES

1 cup (2 sticks) butter or margarine,
    softened
½ cup sugar
1 teaspoon vanilla extract
1¾ cups all-purpose flour

1 cup finely chopped walnuts
1 package (6 oz.) HERSHEY'S
    KISSES Chocolates, unwrapped
Powdered sugar

In large mixer bowl, beat butter, sugar, and vanilla until light and fluffy. Add flour and nuts; beat on low speed of electric mixer until well blended. Cover; refrigerate dough 1 to 2 hours or until firm enough to handle. Heat oven to 375°F. Using approximately 1 tablespoon of dough for each cookie, shape dough around each chocolate piece; roll to make ball. (Be sure to cover each chocolate piece completely.) Place on ungreased cookie sheet. Bake 10 to 12 minutes or until cookies are set but not brown. Cool slightly; remove to wire rack. While still slightly warm, roll in powdered sugar. Cool completely. Store in tightly covered container. Roll again in powdered sugar just before serving. About 3 dozen cookies.

NOTE: For variety, sift together 1 tablespoon HERSHEY'S Cocoa with ⅓ cup powdered sugar. Roll warm cookies in cocoa mixture.

PEANUT BUTTER CHIP OATMEAL COOKIES

1 cup (2 sticks) margarine, softened
¼ cup shortening
2 cups packed light brown sugar
1 tablespoon milk
2 teaspoons vanilla extract
l egg
2 cups all-purpose flour

1⅔ cups (10-oz. pkg.) REESE'S
   Peanut Butter Chips
1½ cups quick-cooking or regular
   rolled oats
½ cup chopped walnuts
½ teaspoon baking soda
½ teaspoon salt

Heat oven to 375°F. In large mixer bowl, beat margarine, shortening, brown sugar, milk, vanilla and egg until well blended. Mix in remaining ingredients. Drop dough by rounded teaspoonfuls about 2 inches apart onto ungreased cookie sheet. Bake until light brown, 10 to 12 minutes for soft cookies, 12 to 14 minutes for crisp cookies. Remove from cookie sheet to wire rack. Cool completely. Store tightly covered. About 6 dozen cookies.

PEANUT BUTTER CHOCOLATE CHUNK COOKIES

¼ cup (½ stick) butter or margarine,
   softened
¼ cup shortening
½ cup REESE'S Creamy Peanut
   Butter
½ cup granulated sugar
½ cup packed light brown sugar

1 egg
1¼ cups all-purpose flour
¾ teaspoon baking soda
½ teaspoon baking powder
1¾ cups (10-oz. pkg.) HERSHEY'S
   Semi-Sweet Chocolate Chunks

Heat oven to 375°F. In large mixer bowl, beat butter, shortening, peanut butter, granulated sugar, brown sugar and egg until creamy. Blend in flour, baking soda and baking powder. Stir in chocolate chunks. Shape into 1-inch balls; place on ungreased cookie sheet. With fork dipped in sugar, flatten slightly in crisscross pattern. Bake 9 to 11 minutes or just until set. Cool slightly; remove from cookie sheet to wire rack. Cool completely. About 3 dozen cookies.

REESE'S CHEWY CHOCOLATE PAN COOKIES

1¼ cups (2½ sticks) butter or
   margarine, softened
2 cups sugar
2 eggs
2 teaspoons vanilla extract
2 cups all-purpose flour

¾ cup HERSHEY'S Cocoa
1 teaspoon baking soda
½ teaspoon salt
1⅔ cups (10-oz. pkg.) REESE'S
   Peanut Butter Chips

Heat oven to 350°F. Grease 15½x10½x1-inch jelly-roll pan. In large mixer bowl, beat butter and sugar until light and fluffy. Add eggs and vanilla; beat well. Stir together flour, cocoa, baking soda and salt; gradually blend into butter mixture. Stir in peanut butter chips. Spread batter into prepared pan. Bake 20 minutes or until set. Cool completely in pan on wire rack; cut into bars. About 4 dozen bars.

REESE'S PIECES CHOCOLATE COOKIES

½ cup (1 stick) margarine or
   shortening
1 cup sugar
1 egg
1 teaspoon vanilla extract
1½ cups all-purpose flour

⅓ cup HERSHEY'S Cocoa
½ teaspoon baking soda
½ teaspoon salt
¼ cup milk
1¼ cups REESE'S PIECES Candy,
   divided

Heat oven to 375°F. In large mixer bowl, beat margarine, sugar, egg and vanilla until well blended. Stir together flour, cocoa, baking soda and salt; add alternately with milk to margarine mixture, beating until well blended. Stir in ¾ cup candies. Drop by teaspoonful onto ungreased cookie sheet. Place 2 or 3 of remaining candies on top of each cookie near center. Bake 10 to 11 minutes or until soft-set (do not overbake). Cool 1 minute; remove from cookie sheet to wire rack. Cool completely. About 3½ dozen cookies.

PEANUT BUTTER CUP COOKIES

½ cup (1 stick) butter or margarine,
   softened
½ cup REESE'S Creamy Peanut
   Butter
½ cup packed light brown sugar
¼ cup granulated sugar
1 egg
1⅔ cups all-purpose flour

1 teaspoon baking soda
1 egg white
1 tablespoon water
1 cup crushed corn flakes
About 40 (14-oz. pkg.) REESE'S
   Peanut Butter Cups Miniatures,
   unwrapped

Heat oven to 375°F. In large mixer bowl, beat butter, peanut butter, brown sugar and granulated sugar until light and fluffy; blend in egg. Stir together flour and baking soda; add to butter mixture. Shape dough into 1-inch balls. Stir together egg white and water; beat with fork until foamy. Roll balls in egg white mixture, then in crushed cereal. Place on ungreased cookie sheet; press with thumb or finger tips in center making an impression about 1-inch wide. Bake 8 to 10 minutes or until cookies are set. Remove from oven; immediately press peanut butter cup onto each cookie. Cool 1 minute; carefully remove from cookie sheet to wire rack. Cool completely. About 3½ dozen cookies.

SKOR & CHOCOLATE CHIPS COOKIES

1 cup (2 sticks) butter, softened
¾ cup granulated sugar
¾ cup packed light brown sugar
1 teaspoon vanilla extract
2 eggs
2¼ cups all-purpose flour

1 teaspoon baking soda
½ teaspoon salt
1 cup HERSHEY'S Semi-Sweet
   Chocolate Chips
1 cup finely chopped SKOR Toffee
   Candy Bars (about 4 bars)

Heat oven to 375°F. In large mixer bowl, beat butter, granulated sugar, brown sugar and vanilla until light and fluffy. Add eggs; beat well. Stir together flour, baking soda and salt; gradually beat into butter mixture. Stir in chocolate chips and chopped toffee bars. Drop by teaspoonfuls onto ungreased cookie sheet. Bake 8 to 10 minutes or until lightly browned. Cool slightly; remove from cookie sheet to wire rack. Cool completely. 6 dozen cookies.

PEANUT BUTTER TEMPTATIONS

About 40 (14-oz. pkg.) REESE'S Peanut Butter Cups Miniatures, unwrapped
1/2 cup (1 stick) butter or margarine, softened
1/2 cup packed light brown sugar
1/2 cup granulated sugar
1/2 cup REESE'S Creamy Peanut Butter
1 egg
1/2 teaspoon vanilla extract
1 1/2 cups all-purpose flour
3/4 teaspoon baking soda
1/2 teaspoon salt

Heat oven to 375°F. Paper-line 40 small muffin cups (1 3/4-inches in diameter). In large mixer bowl, beat butter, brown sugar, granulated sugar, peanut butter, egg and vanilla until light and fluffy. Stir together flour, baking soda and salt; add to butter mixture, beating until well blended. Shape dough into 1-inch balls; place one in each prepared muffin cup. Do not flatten. Bake 10 to 12 minutes until puffed and lightly browned; remove from oven. Immediately press peanut butter cup onto each cookie. Cool completely in muffin cups. About 3 1/2 dozen cookies.

QUICK & CHEWY CHOCOLATE DROPS

1 package (8 oz.) HERSHEY'S Semi-Sweet Baking Chocolate, broken into pieces
1/4 cup (1/2 stick) butter or margarine, softened
1/2 cup sugar
1 egg
1 1/2 teaspoons vanilla extract
1/2 cup all-purpose flour
1/4 teaspoon baking powder
1/2 cup chopped nuts (optional)

Heat oven to 350°F. In small microwave-safe bowl, place chocolate. Microwave at HIGH (100%) 1 1/2 to 2 minutes or until chocolate is melted when stirred; cool slightly. In large mixer bowl, beat butter and sugar until well blended. Add egg and vanilla; beat well. Blend in melted chocolate, flour and baking powder. Stir in nuts, if desired. Drop by rounded teaspoonfuls onto ungreased cookie sheet. Bake 8 to 10 minutes or until almost set. Cool slightly; remove from cookie sheet to wire rack. Cool completely. About 2 dozen cookies.

REESE'S PEANUT BLOSSOMS

1/2 cup (1 stick) butter or margarine
1 cup REESE'S Peanut Butter Chips
2/3 cup packed light brown sugar
1 egg
3/4 teaspoon vanilla extract
1 1/3 cups all-purpose flour
3/4 teaspoon baking soda
1/2 cup finely chopped nuts
Granulated sugar
1 bag (9 oz.) HERSHEY'S KISSES Chocolates, unwrapped

Heat oven to 350°F. In saucepan over low heat, place butter and peanut butter chips; heat, stirring constantly, until melted. Pour mixture into large mixer bowl; add brown sugar, egg and vanilla, beating until well blended. Stir in flour, baking soda and nuts, blending well. Shape dough into 1-inch ball. Roll in granulated sugar; place on ungreased cookie sheet. Bake 10 to 12 minutes or until lightly browned. Remove from oven; immediately place chocolate piece on top of each cookie, pressing down so cookie cracks around edges. Remove from cookie sheet to wire rack. Cool completely. About 4 dozen cookies.

REESE'S PEANUT BUTTER CUP COOKIES

¾ cup REESE'S Creamy Peanut
  Butter
½ cup shortening
⅓ cup granulated sugar
⅓ cup packed light brown sugar
1 egg
2 tablespoons milk

1 teaspoon vanilla extract
1⅓ cups all-purpose flour
1 teaspoon baking soda
Granulated sugar
About 30 REESE'S Peanut Butter
  Cups Miniatures, unwrapped

Heat oven to 350°F. In large mixer bowl, beat peanut butter, shortening, granulated sugar and brown sugar. Add egg, milk and vanilla; beat well. Stir together flour and baking soda; gradually add to sugar mixture, blending thoroughly. Shape dough into 1½-inch balls; roll in granulated sugar. Place on ungreased cookie sheet. Bake 10 to 12 minutes or until just set; remove from oven. Immediately place peanut butter cup on top of each cookie, pressing down so cookie cracks around edges. Cool slightly; remove from cookie sheet to wire rack. Cool completely. About 2½ dozen cookies.

PEANUT BUTTER CHIP AND JELLY THUMBPRINT COOKIES

1 cup (2 sticks) butter or margarine,
  softened
1¾ cups packed light brown sugar
2 eggs
2 teaspoons vanilla extract
3 cups all-purpose flour

1 teaspoon baking powder
1 teaspoon salt
1⅔ cups (10-oz. pkg.) REESE'S
  Peanut Butter Chips, divided
1½ cups quick-cooking oats
¾ cup jelly or preserves

In large mixer bowl, beat butter and brown sugar. Add eggs and vanilla; beat well. Stir together flour, baking powder and salt; gradually add to butter mixture. Measure ⅓ cup peanut butter chips; set aside. Stir oats and remaining 1⅓ cups peanut butter chips into butter mixture. Cover; refrigerate several hours or until firm enough to shape. Heat oven to 400°F. Shape dough into 1-inch balls; place on ungreased cookie sheet. Press thumb or back of spoon gently in center of each cookie. Bake 7 to 9 minutes or until lightly browned. Cool slightly; remove from cookie sheet to wire rack. (Press thumb gently in center of each cookie, while warm, if deeper indentation is desired.) Cool completely; fill center of each cookie with about ½ teaspoon jelly. Top each cookie with reserved peanut butter chips. About 5 dozen cookies.

REESE'S CHEWY CHOCOLATE COOKIES

2 cups all-purpose flour
¾ cup HERSHEY'S Cocoa
1 teaspoon baking soda
½ teaspoon salt
1¼ cups (2½ sticks) butter or
  margarine, softened

2 cups sugar
2 eggs
2 teaspoons vanilla extract
1⅔ cups (10-oz. pkg.) REESE'S
  Peanut Butter Chips

Heat oven to 350°F. Stir together flour, cocoa, baking soda and salt. In large mixer bowl, beat butter and sugar until light and fluffy. Add eggs and vanilla; beat well. Gradually add flour mixture, beating well. Stir in peanut butter chips. Drop by rounded teaspoonfuls onto ungreased cookie sheet. Bake 8 to 9 minutes. (Do not overbake; cookies will be soft. They will puff while baking and flatten while cooling.) Cool slightly; remove from cookie sheet to wire rack. Cool completely. About 4½ dozen cookies.

PAN RECIPE: Spread batter in greased 15½x10½x1-inch jelly-roll pan. Bake at 350°F. 20 minutes or until set. Cool completely in pan on wire rack; cut into bars. About 4 dozen bars.

TROPICAL NUT CRISPS

¾ cup (1½ sticks) butter or
    margarine, softened
1 cup sugar
¼ cup light corn syrup
1 egg
½ teaspoon orange, lemon or
    pineapple extract
½ teaspoon vanilla extract

1⅔ cups (10-oz. pkg.) HERSHEY'S
    Vanilla Milk Chips, divided
2½ cups all-purpose flour
2 teaspoons baking soda
¼ teaspoon salt
1 to 1¼ cups finely ground nuts
VANILLA MILK CHIP GLAZE (recipe
    follows)

In large mixer bowl, beat butter and sugar until light and fluffy. Add corn syrup, egg, orange and vanilla extracts; blend well. In small microwave-safe bowl, place 1 cup vanilla milk chips. Microwave at HIGH (100%) 1 minute or until smooth when stirred vigorously; blend into butter mixture. Stir together flour, baking soda and salt; add to vanilla mixture, blending well. Refrigerate 1 hour or until dough is firm enough to handle. Heat oven to 350°F. Shape dough into 1-inch balls; roll in nuts, pressing nuts into dough lightly. Place on ungreased cookie sheet. Bake 8 to 10 minutes or until golden around edges. Cool several minutes; remove from cookie sheet to wire rack. Cool completely. Drizzle VANILLA MILK CHIP GLAZE over each cookie. About 5 dozen cookies.

VANILLA MILK CHIP GLAZE: In small microwave-safe bowl, place remaining ⅔ cup vanilla milk chips and 1½ teaspoons shortening. Microwave at HIGH (100%) 1 minute; stir until smooth when stirred.

PRELUDE THUMBPRINT COOKIES

1 cup (2 sticks) butter or margarine,
    softened
1⅓ cups sugar
2 eggs
¼ cup milk
2 teaspoons vanilla extract
2 cups all-purpose flour
⅔ cup HERSHEY'S Cocoa

½ teaspoon salt
⅔ cup slivered almonds, chopped
ORANGE FILLING (recipe follows)
6 SYMPHONY Milk Chocolate Bars
    or SYMPHONY Milk Chocolate
    Bars With Almonds & Toffee
    Chips (1.4 oz. each), broken into
    pieces*

In large mixer bowl, beat butter, sugar, eggs, milk and vanilla until well blended. Stir together flour, cocoa and salt; add to butter mixture, mixing until well blended. Refrigerate dough 1 to 2 hours or until firm enough to handle. Heat oven to 350°F. Lightly grease cookie sheet. Shape dough into 1-inch balls; roll in almonds. Place on prepared cookie sheet; press thumb gently in center of each cookie. Bake 10 to 12 minutes or until set. Cool slightly; press thumb again into center of each cookie. Remove to wire rack to cool completely. Spoon about ¼ teaspoon ORANGE FILLING in each thumbprint. Gently press chocolate bar piece into filling of each cookie. About 4 dozen cookies.

ORANGE FILLING

1 cup powdered sugar
2 tablespoons butter or margarine,
    softened
4 teaspoons milk

½ teaspoon freshly grated orange peel
½ teaspoon vanilla extract
Few drops red and yellow food color
    (optional)

In small mixer bowl, combine powdered sugar, butter, milk, orange peel and vanilla; beat until smooth. Stir in red and yellow food color, if desired.

* 1 SYMPHONY Milk Chocolate Bar or Milk Chocolate Bar with Almonds & Toffee Chips (7 oz.) may be substituted.

TIGER STRIPED PEANUT BUTTER COOKIES

¾ cup (1½ sticks) butter or
   margarine, softened
1¼ cups REESE'S Creamy or
   Crunchy Peanut Butter
½ cup granulated sugar
½ cup packed light brown sugar

1 egg
2 tablespoons milk
1 teaspoon vanilla extract
2 cups all-purpose flour
¼ teaspoon baking soda
CHOCOLATE GLAZE (recipe follows)

In large mixer bowl, beat butter, peanut butter, granulated sugar and brown sugar until well blended. Add egg, milk and vanilla; beat until well blended. Add flour and baking soda; beat until smooth. Refrigerate 1 to 2 hours or until firm enough to roll.* Heat oven to 375°F. Roll small portion of dough at a time on lightly floured board or between 2 pieces of wax paper to ¼-inch thickness. Cut into desired shapes with cookie cutters; place on ungreased cookie sheet. Bake 5 to 7 minutes or until edges are lightly browned. Cool slightly; remove to wire rack. Cool completely. Drizzle with CHOCOLATE GLAZE. About 6 dozen cookies.

CHOCOLATE GLAZE: In small microwave-safe bowl, place 1 cup HERSHEY'S Semi-Sweet Chocolate Chips and 1 tablespoon shortening. Microwave at HIGH (100%) 1 to 1½ minutes or until smooth when stirred. About ½ cup glaze.

*SLICE AND BAKE COOKIES: Shape mixture into 2 rolls, 2-inches in diameter. Wrap in plastic wrap; refrigerate several hours or overnight. Unwrap; cut each roll into ¼-inch slices. Bake as directed above.

DEEP DARK CHOCOLATE COOKIES

¾ cup (1½ sticks) butter or
   margarine, softened
¾ cup granulated sugar
½ cup packed light brown sugar
1 teaspoon vanilla extract
2 eggs
1¾ cups all-purpose flour

½ cup HERSHEY'S Cocoa
¾ teaspoon baking soda
½ teaspoon baking powder
¼ teaspoon salt
1 cup HERSHEY'S Semi-Sweet
   Chocolate Chips
½ cup chopped nuts

Heat oven to 375°F. In large mixer bowl, beat butter, granulated sugar, brown sugar and vanilla with an electric mixer on medium speed about 2 minutes or until well blended. Add eggs; beat well. Stir together flour, cocoa, baking soda, baking powder and salt; gradually add to butter mixture, beating just until blended. Stir in chocolate chips and nuts. Drop by heaping teaspoonfuls onto cookie sheet. Bake 7 minutes or until set. Cool 1 minute; remove from cookie sheet to wire rack. Cool completely. About 4 dozen cookies.

SYMPHONY MILK CHOCOLATE MACADAMIA COOKIES

1 SYMPHONY Milk Chocolate Bar or
  Milk Chocolate Bar with Almonds
  & Toffee Chips (7 oz.)
6 tablespoons butter or margarine,
  softened
½ cup granulated sugar
¼ cup packed light brown sugar

½ teaspoon vanilla extract
1 egg
1 cup all-purpose flour
½ teaspoon baking soda
1 cup coarsely chopped macadamia
  nuts

Heat oven to 350°F. Cut chocolate bar into ¼-inch pieces; set aside. In large mixer bowl, beat butter, granulated sugar, brown sugar and vanilla until well blended. Add egg; beat well. Stir together flour and baking soda; blend into butter mixture. Stir in macadamia nuts and chocolate pieces. Drop by heaping tablespoonfuls onto ungreased cookie sheet. Bake 10 to 12 minutes or until lightly browned. Cool slightly; remove from cookie sheet to wire rack. Cool completely. About 2 dozen cookies.

BUTTERSCOTCH CHEWY COOKIES

¾ cup (1½ sticks) butter or
  margarine, softened
1 cup packed light brown sugar
¼ cup light corn syrup
1 egg
1⅔ cups (10-oz. pkg.) HERSHEY'S
  Butterscotch Chips, divided

2½ cups all-purpose flour
2 teaspoons baking soda
¼ teaspoon salt
1 to 1¼ cups finely ground nuts
BUTTERSCOTCH CHIP DRIZZLE
  (recipe follows)

In large mixer bowl, beat butter and sugar until light and fluffy. Add corn syrup and egg; blend well. In small microwave-safe bowl, microwave 1 cup butterscotch chips at HIGH (100%) 1 minute or until smooth when stirred; blend into butter mixture. In separate bowl, stir together flour, baking soda and salt; add to butterscotch mixture, blending well. Refrigerate 1 hour or until dough is firm enough to handle. Heat oven to 350°F. Roll dough into 1-inch balls; roll in nuts, pressing nuts into dough lightly. Place on cookie sheet. Bake 8 to 10 minutes or until golden around the edges. Cool several minutes; remove from cookie sheet to wire rack. Cool completely. Drizzle with BUTTERSCOTCH CHIP DRIZZLE. About 5 dozen cookies.

BUTTERSCOTCH CHIP DRIZZLE: In small microwave-safe bowl; place remaining ⅔ cups butterscotch chips and 1½ teaspoons shortening. Microwave at HIGH (100%) 1 minute; stir until chips are melted and mixture is smooth.

HALLOWEEN SANDWICH COOKIES

½ cup (1 stick) butter or margarine,
  softened
¾ cup sugar
1 egg
1 tablespoon milk
½ teaspoon vanilla extract
1½ cups all-purpose flour
⅓ cup HERSHEY'S Cocoa

½ teaspoon baking powder
⅛ teaspoon salt
1 HERSHEY'S Milk Chocolate Bar (7
  oz.), broken into pieces
9 to 12 large marshmallows, cut in
  half
DECORATOR FROSTING (recipe
  follows)

In large mixer bowl, beat butter, sugar, egg, milk and vanilla until well blended. In bowl, stir together flour, cocoa, baking powder and salt; add to butter mixture, mixing until well blended. Divide dough into quarters; wrap tightly. Refrigerate 2 to 3 hours. Heat oven to 325°F. On lightly floured surface, roll out dough, one-fourth at a time, to ⅛-inch thickness. With ghost or cat shaped cookie cutters, cut dough. Place cookies 1 inch apart on ungreased cookie sheet. Bake 8 to 10 minutes or until firm. Remove from cookie sheet to wire rack; cool completely. Place chocolate piece and marshmallow on flat side of 1 cookie; place on paper towel. Microwave at HIGH (100%) 15 to 30 seconds or until marshmallow puffs. Top with matching cookie; press down slightly. Repeat with remaining cookies. Decorate with DECORATOR FROSTING, if desired. About 1½ dozen sandwich cookies.

DECORATOR FROSTING: In small mixer bowl, combine 3 tablespoons water and 1 tablespoon meringue powder. Add 1¼ to 1½ cups powdered sugar and ⅛ teaspoon vanilla extract; beat on high speed of electric mixer until stiff.

HERSHEY'S GREAT AMERICAN CHOCOLATE CHIP COOKIES

2¼ cups all-purpose flour
1 teaspoon baking soda
½ teaspoon salt
1 cup (2 sticks) butter, softened
¾ cup granulated sugar
¾ cup packed light brown sugar

1 teaspoon vanilla extract
2 eggs
2 cups (12-oz. pkg.) HERSHEY'S
  Semi-Sweet Chocolate Chips
1 cup chopped nuts (optional)

Heat oven to 375°F. In bowl, stir together flour, baking soda and salt. In large mixer bowl, beat butter, granulated sugar, brown sugar and vanilla until creamy. Add eggs; beat well. Gradually add flour mixture, beating well. Stir in chocolate chips and nuts, if desired. Drop by rounded teaspoonfuls onto ungreased cookie sheet. Bake 9 to 11 minutes or until lightly browned. Cool slightly; remove from cookie sheet to wire rack. Cool completely. About 6 dozen cookies.

PAN RECIPE: Spread batter in greased 15½x10½x1-inch jelly roll pan. Bake at 375°F. 20 minutes or until lightly browned. Cool completely; cut into bars. About 4 dozen bars.

DOUBLE CHOCOLATE HITS

⅔ cup butter or margarine, softened
1 cup sugar
1 egg
1 teaspoon vanilla extract
½ cup HERSHEY'S Cocoa
½ cup buttermilk or sour milk*

1¾ cups all-purpose flour
½ teaspoon baking soda
½ teaspoon salt
1 cup HERSHEY'S MINI CHIPS
    Semi-Sweet Chocolate

Heat oven to 350°F. In large mixer bowl, beat butter, sugar, egg and vanilla until well blended. In small bowl, stir cocoa and buttermilk until smooth; add to butter mixture. Stir together flour, baking soda and salt; add to butter mixture, beating just until blended. Stir in small chocolate chips. Drop dough by teaspoonfuls onto ungreased cookie sheet. Bake 8 to 10 minutes or until center of cookies is not quite set. Remove from cookie sheet to wire rack. Cool completely. About 3½ dozen cookies.

* To sour milk: Use 1½ teaspoons white vinegar plus milk to equal ½ cup.

CHEWY CHOCOLATE OATMEAL COOKIES

½ cup HERSHEY'S Cocoa
½ cup (1 stick) butter or margarine,
    melted
1 can (14 oz.) sweetened condensed
    milk
2 eggs, beaten
2 teaspoons vanilla extract

1½ cups quick-cooking rolled oats
1 cup all-purpose biscuit baking mix
¼ teaspoon salt
1⅔ cups (10-oz.pkg.) HERSHEY'S
    Vanilla Milk Chips
1⅔ cups (10-oz.pkg.) REESE'S Peanut
    Butter Chips

Heat oven to 350°F. Lightly grease cookie sheet. In large bowl, stir together cocoa and butter until mixture is smooth. Stir in sweetened condensed milk, eggs, vanilla extract, oats, baking mix, salt, vanilla milk chips and peanut butter chips until well blended. Let batter rest 10 minutes; drop by heaping teaspoonfuls onto prepared cookie sheet. Bake 7 to 9 minutes or until tops begin to dry (do not overbake). Cool 5 minutes; remove from cookie sheet to wire rack. Cool completely. Store in airtight container. About 4 dozen cookies.

EASY CHOCOLATE CHUNK COOKIES

1 package (15 oz.) sugar cookie mix

1 HERSHEY'S Milk Chocolate Bar (7
    oz.) or SPECIAL DARK
    Chocolate Bar (7 oz.)

Heat oven to 375°F. Prepare cookie dough according to package directions; set aside. Break chocolate bar into ½-inch pieces; stir into cookie dough. Drop dough by ¼ cupfuls 2 inches apart on ungreased cookie sheet. Bake 12 to 14 minutes or just until lightly browned; cool on cookie sheet about 1 minute. Remove from cookie sheet to wire rack; cool completely. About 10 large cookies.

PEANUT BUTTER VARIATION: Stir in 1 cup REESE'S PIECES or 1 cup REESE'S Peanut Butter Chips instead of chocolate bar pieces.

BROWNIES AND BARS
HERSHEY'S VANILLA CHIP BROWNIES

4 eggs
1¼ cups sugar
¼ cup (½ stick) butter or margarine,
    melted
2 teaspoons vanilla extract
1⅓ cups all-purpose flour

⅔ cup HERSHEY'S Cocoa
1 teaspoon baking powder
½ teaspoon salt
1⅔ cups (10-oz. pkg.) HERSHEY'S
    Vanilla Milk Chips

Heat oven to 350°F. Grease 13x9x2-inch baking pan. In large mixer bowl, beat eggs until foamy; gradually beat in sugar. Blend in butter and vanilla extract. Stir together flour, cocoa, baking powder and salt; add to egg mixture, blending thoroughly. Stir in vanilla milk chips. Spread batter into prepared pan. Bake 25 to 30 minutes or until brownies begin to pull away from sides of pan. Cool completely in pan on wire rack. Cut into bars. About 32 brownies.

REESE'S BROWNIES

¾ cup HERSHEY'S Cocoa
½ teaspoon baking soda
⅔ cup butter or margarine, melted
    and divided
½ cup boiling water
2 cups sugar

2 eggs
1½ cups all-purpose flour
1 teaspoon vanilla extract
¼ teaspoon salt
1⅔ cups (10-oz. pkg.) REESE'S
    Peanut Butter Chips

Heat oven to 350°F. Grease 13x9x2-inch baking pan or two 8-inch square baking pans. In large bowl, stir together cocoa and baking soda; stir in ⅓ cup butter. Add boiling water; stir until mixture thickens. Stir in sugar, eggs and remaining ⅓ cup butter; stir until smooth. Add flour, vanilla and salt; blend completely. Stir in peanut butter chips. Pour into prepared pan. Bake 35 to 40 minutes for rectangular pan, 30 to 35 minutes for square pans or until brownies begin to pull away from sides of pan. Cool completely in pan on wire rack. Cut into squares. About 36 brownies.

HERSHEY'S PREMIUM DOUBLY CHOCOLATE BROWNIES

¾ cup HERSHEY'S Cocoa
½ teaspoon baking soda
⅔ cup butter or margarine, melted
    and divided
½ cup boiling water
2 cups sugar
2 eggs

1⅓ cups all-purpose flour
1 teaspoon vanilla extract
¼ teaspoon salt
1¾ cups (10-oz.pkg.) HERSHEY'S
    Semi-Sweet Chocolate Chunks
½ cup coarsely chopped nuts
    (optional)

Heat oven to 350°F. Grease 13x9x2-inch baking pan. In large bowl, stir together cocoa and baking soda; blend in ⅓ cup butter. Add water; stir until mixture thickens. Stir in sugar, eggs and remaining ⅓ cup butter; stir until smooth. Add flour, vanilla and salt; blend well. Stir in chocolate chunks and nuts, if desired. Spread batter into prepared pan. Bake 35 to 40 minutes or until brownies begin to pull away from sides of pan. Cool completely in pan on wire rack. Cut into bars. About 36 brownies.

BROWNIE BITES WITH MAGIC FROSTING

¾ cup HERSHEY'S Cocoa
⅔ cup vegetable oil
2 cups sugar
4 eggs
2 teaspoons vanilla extract
1¼ cups all-purpose flour

1 teaspoon baking powder
½ teaspoon salt
1⅔ cups (10-oz. pkg.) REESE'S
    Peanut Butter Chips or
    HERSHEY'S Vanilla Milk Chips,
    divided

Heat oven to 350°F. On cookie sheets, place about 40 foil baking cups (2-inches in diameter). In large bowl, stir together cocoa and vegetable oil until smooth; stir in sugar. Beat in eggs and vanilla; stir in flour, baking powder and salt. Stir in 1 cup peanut butter chips, reserving remaining ⅔ cup for frosting. Drop mixture by rounded tablespoonfuls into baking cups. Bake 15 to 18 minutes or just until set and small cracks appear on surface. Remove from oven; immediately place about 6 reserved peanut butter chips on center of each brownie. Let stand several minutes to soften; swirl melted chips with knife or spatula. About 3 dozen brownies.

HERSHEY'S BROWNIES

½ cup (1 stick) butter or margarine
2½ bars (2½ oz.) HERSHEY'S
    Unsweetened Baking Chocolate,
    broken into pieces
2 eggs
1 cup sugar

1 teaspoon vanilla extract
½ cup all-purpose flour
¼ teaspoon baking powder
¼ teaspoon salt
½ cup chopped nuts

Heat oven to 350°F. Grease 8-inch square pan. In small saucepan over low heat, melt butter; remove from heat. Stir in baking chocolate pieces until melted; set aside to cool. In small mixer bowl, beat eggs slightly; gradually add sugar, beating well. Add chocolate mixture and vanilla. Stir together flour, baking powder and salt; blend into chocolate mixture. Stir in nuts. Pour into prepared pan. Bake 30 to 35 minutes or until brownies begin to pull away from sides of pan. Cool completely in pan on wire rack. Cut into squares. About 16 brownies.

THREE GREAT TASTES BLOND BROWNIES

2 cups packed light brown sugar
1 cup (2 sticks) butter or margarine,
    melted
2 eggs
2 teaspoons vanilla extract
2 cups all-purpose flour
1 teaspoon salt

⅔ cup (of each) HERSHEY'S Semi-
    Sweet Chocolate Chips, REESE'S
    Peanut Butter Chips, and
    HERSHEY'S Vanilla Milk Chips
CHOCOLATE CHIP DRIZZLE (recipe
    follows)

Heat oven to 350°F. Grease 15½x10½x1-inch jelly-roll pan. In large bowl, stir together brown sugar and butter; beat in eggs and vanilla until smooth. Add flour and salt, beating just until blended; stir in chocolate, peanut butter and vanilla milk chips. Spread batter into prepared pan. Bake 25 to 30 minutes or until wooden pick inserted in center comes out clean. Cool completely; cut into bars. With tines of fork, drizzle CHOCOLATE CHIP DRIZZLE randomly over bars. About 6 dozen bars.

CHOCOLATE CHIP DRIZZLE: In small microwave-safe bowl, place ¼ cup HERSHEY'S Semi-Sweet Chocolate Chips and ¼ teaspoon shortening. Microwave at HIGH (100%) 30 seconds to 1 minute; stir until chips are melted and mixture is smooth.

QUICK & EASY CHOCOLATE BROWNIES

½ cup sugar
¼ cup evaporated milk
¼ cup (½ stick) butter or margarine
1 package (8 oz.) HERSHEY'S Semi-
   Sweet Baking Chocolate, broken
   into pieces

2 eggs
1 teaspoon vanilla extract
¾ cup all-purpose flour
¼ teaspoon baking soda
¼ teaspoon salt
¾ cup chopped nuts (optional)

Heat oven to 325°F. Grease 9-inch square baking pan. In medium saucepan, combine sugar, evaporated milk and butter. Cook over medium heat, stirring constantly, until mixture boils; remove from heat. Add chocolate, stirring until melted; beat in eggs and vanilla. Stir in flour, baking soda, salt and nuts, if desired, until well blended; pour into prepared pan. Bake 30 to 35 minutes or until brownies just begin to pull away from sides of pan. Cool completely in pan on wire rack. Cut into squares. Frost, if desired. About 16 brownies.

QUICK & EASY FUDGEY BROWNIES

4 bars (4 oz.) HERSHEY'S
   Unsweetened Baking Chocolate,
   broken into pieces
¾ cup (1½ sticks) butter or margarine
2 cups sugar
3 eggs

1½ teaspoons vanilla extract
1 cup all-purpose flour
1 cup chopped nuts (optional)
QUICK & EASY CHOCOLATE
   FROSTING (optional) (page 12)

Heat oven to 350°F. Grease 13x9x2-inch baking pan. In large microwave-safe bowl, place chocolate and butter. Microwave at HIGH (100%) 1½ to 2 minutes or until chocolate is melted and mixture is smooth when stirred. Add sugar; stir with spoon until well blended. Add eggs and vanilla; mix well. Add flour and nuts, if desired; stir until well blended. Spread into prepared pan. Bake 30 to 35 minutes or until wooden pick inserted in center comes out almost clean. Cool in pan on wire rack. Frost with QUICK & EASY CHOCOLATE FROSTING, if desired. Cut into squares. About 24 brownies.

FUDGEY CHOCOLATE BROWNIES

1 cup (2 sticks) butter or margarine
4 bars (4 oz.) HERSHEY'S
   Unsweetened Baking Chocolate,
   broken into pieces
2 cups sugar

4 eggs
1 cup all-purpose flour
1 teaspoon vanilla extract
¼ teaspoon salt
½ cup chopped nuts (optional)

Heat oven to 350°F. Grease 13x9x2-inch baking pan. In large microwave-safe bowl, place butter and chocolate. Microwave at HIGH (100%) 1 to 1½ minutes or until chocolate is melted and mixture is smooth when stirred; stir in sugar. Add eggs, one at a time, beating with spoon until blended. Stir in flour, vanilla and salt until blended. Stir in nuts, if desired. Spread mixture evenly into prepared pan. Bake 30 to 35 minutes or until wooden pick inserted in center comes out clean. Cool completely in pan on wire rack. Cut into bars. About 3 dozen brownies.

Saucepan Method: Heat oven and grease pan as directed. In 3-quart saucepan, over very low heat, melt butter and chocolate, stirring frequently. Remove from heat; stir in remaining ingredients. Bake as directed above.

TRIPLE LAYER BROWNIES

2 cups sugar
2 cups all-purpose flour
⅔ cup HERSHEY'S Cocoa
1 teaspoon baking powder
½ teaspoon salt
¾ cup (1½ sticks) butter or margarine
4 eggs

2 teaspoons vanilla extract
2 cups miniature marshmallows
1⅔ cups (10-oz. pkg.) REESE'S
  Peanut Butter Chips
2 tablespoons shortening
3 cups crisp rice cereal

Heat oven to 350°F. Grease 13x9x2-inch baking pan. In large bowl, stir together sugar, flour, cocoa, baking powder and salt. With pastry blender, cut in butter until mixture resembles coarse crumbs; set aside. In separate bowl, lightly beat eggs and vanilla. Add dry mixture to egg mixture; beat until ingredients are well blended. Spread batter into prepared pan. Bake 25 minutes; remove from oven. Sprinkle marshmallows evenly over brownies, covering entire surface; return to oven. Bake additional 5 minutes; remove from oven. Cool in pan 10 minutes. In top of double boiler, over hot, not boiling, water, combine peanut butter chips and shortening; stir until melted. Add rice cereal; stir until thoroughly coated. Immediately spread over top of marshmallows. Cool completely in pan on wire rack. Cut into squares. About 32 squares.

CHOCOLATE CHEESE BROWNIES

1 cup (2 sticks) butter or margarine,
  softened and divided
1 package (3 oz.) cream cheese,
  softened
1 cup sugar
1 egg
1 teaspoon vanilla extract

2 cups (12-oz. pkg.) HERSHEY'S
  Semi-Sweet Chocolate Chips or
  MINI CHIPS Semi-Sweet
  Chocolate
2¼ cups all-purpose flour
1 teaspoon baking powder
½ cup chopped walnuts (optional)

Heat oven to 350°F. Grease 13x9x2-inch baking pan. In large mixer bowl, blend ¾ cup (1½ sticks) butter and cream cheese. Gradually add sugar; beat until light and fluffy. Add egg and vanilla; beat well. In small saucepan over low heat, melt remaining ¼ cup (½ stick) butter and chocolate chips, stirring occasionally; gradually add to cream cheese mixture, blending well. Stir together flour and baking powder; blend into chocolate mixture. Stir in nuts, if desired. Spread batter into prepared pan. Bake 30 minutes. Cool completely in pan on wire rack. Cut into bars. About 36 brownies.

CHERRY VANILLA CHIP BROWNIES

½ cup chopped maraschino cherries,
   well drained
⅓ cup butter or margarine, softened
¾ cup sugar
2 eggs
2 tablespoons light corn syrup
1 tablespoon kirsch (cherry brandy) or
   1 teaspoon vanilla extract and 1
   teaspoon almond extract
⅔ cup all-purpose flour

⅓ cup HERSHEY'S European Style
   Cocoa or HERSHEY'S Cocoa
¼ teaspoon baking powder
⅓ cup chopped slivered almonds
1 cup HERSHEY'S Vanilla Milk Chips
VANILLA CHIP DRIZZLE (recipe
   follows, optional)
Maraschino cherry halves, well
   drained (optional)

Heat oven to 350°F. Line 9-inch square baking pan with foil; grease and flour foil. Blot cherries between layers of paper towels; set aside. In small mixer bowl, beat butter, sugar, eggs, corn syrup and brandy until blended. Add flour, cocoa and baking powder; blend until combined. Stir in chopped cherries, almonds and vanilla chips. Pour batter into prepared pan. Bake 25 to 30 minutes or until brownies begin to pull away from sides of pan. Cool completely in pan. Cover; refrigerate until firm. Remove from pan; remove foil. Cut into shapes with cookie cutters, or cut into squares. Garnish with VANILLA CHIP DRIZZLE and maraschino cherry halves, if desired. Refrigerate until drizzle is firm; refrigerate leftovers. About 16 brownies.

VANILLA CHIP DRIZZLE: In small microwave-safe bowl, place ⅔ cup HERSHEY'S Vanilla Milk Chips and 1 teaspoon shortening. Microwave at HIGH (100%) 30 seconds: stir. If necessary, microwave at HIGH additional 15 seconds until chips are melted when stirred. Using tines of fork, drizzle across brownies.

PEANUT BUTTER MARBLE BROWNIES

½ cup (1 stick) butter or margarine
⅓ cup HERSHEY'S Cocoa
3 eggs
1¼ cups sugar, divided
1 teaspoon vanilla extract
½ cup all-purpose flour

½ teaspoon baking powder
¼ teaspoon salt
1 cup REESE'S Peanut Butter Chips,
   divided
1 package (3 oz.) cream cheese,
   softened

Heat oven to 350°F. Grease 9-inch square baking pan. In small saucepan, melt butter; remove from heat. Stir in cocoa, blending well; set aside. In small mixer bowl, beat 2 eggs until foamy; gradually add 1 cup sugar and vanilla, blending well. Stir together flour, baking powder and salt; blend into egg mixture. Add cocoa mixture and ½ cup peanut butter chips; blend well. Remove ½ cup batter; set aside. Spread remaining batter in prepared pan. In microwave-safe bowl, place remaining ½ cup peanut butter chips. Microwave at HIGH (100%) 30 seconds or until chips are melted when stirred. In small mixer bowl, combine cream cheese, remaining ¼ cup sugar and melted peanut butter chips; beat until smooth. Add remaining egg; blend well. Spread cream cheese mixture over chocolate batter. Drop reserved ½ cup chocolate batter by spoonfuls onto cream cheese layer. With knife, gently swirl top of batter into cream cheese layer for marbled effect. Bake 40 to 45 minutes or just until brownies begin to pull away from sides of pan. Cool completely in pan on wire rack. Cut into squares. About 16 brownies.

ULTIMATE DESIGNER BROWNIES

¾ cup HERSHEY'S Cocoa
½ teaspoon baking soda
⅔ cup butter or margarine, melted
   and divided
½ cup boiling water
2 cups sugar
2 eggs
1⅓ cups all-purpose flour
1 teaspoon vanilla extract

¼ teaspoon salt
¾ cup (3½-oz. jar) macadamia nuts,
   coarsely chopped
2 cups (12-oz. pkg.) HERSHEY'S
   Semi-Sweet Chocolate Chips,
   divided
½ teaspoon shortening
VANILLA GLAZE (recipe follows)

Heat oven to 350°F. Grease 13x9x2-inch baking pan or two 8-inch square baking pans. In bowl, stir together cocoa and baking soda; blend in ⅓ cup melted butter. Add boiling water; stir until mixture thickens. Stir in sugar, eggs and remaining ⅓ cup melted butter; stir until smooth. Add flour, vanilla and salt; blend well. Stir in nuts and 1½ cups chocolate chips. Pour into prepared pan. Bake 35 to 40 minutes for rectangular pan, 30 to 35 minutes for square pans or until brownie begins to pull away from sides of the pan. Cool completely. Prepare VANILLA GLAZE. Drizzle VANILLA GLAZE on brownie surface. Cut into triangles. In small microwave-safe bowl, place remaining ½ cup chocolate chips and shortening, Microwave at HIGH (100%) 45 seconds to 1 minute or until softened; stir until smooth. Put mixture into pastry bag fitted with small writing tip. Pipe signature design on each brownie or drizzle over VANILLA GLAZE. About 24 brownies.

VANILLA GLAZE

2 tablespoons butter or margarine
4 teaspoons milk
¼ teaspoon brandy extract

¼ teaspoon rum extract
1 cup powdered sugar

In small saucepan over low heat, melt butter in milk. Remove from heat; add brandy and rum extract. Gradually add powdered sugar, beating with spoon until smooth. About ½ cup glaze.

DEEP DISH BROWNIES

¾ cup (1½ sticks) butter or
   margarine, melted
1½ cups sugar
1½ teaspoons vanilla extract
3 eggs

¾ cup all-purpose flour
½ cup HERSHEY'S Cocoa
½ teaspoon baking powder
½ teaspoon salt

Heat oven to 350°F. Grease 8-inch square baking pan. In bowl, stir together butter, sugar and vanilla. Add eggs; with spoon, beat well. Stir together flour, cocoa, baking powder and salt; gradually add to egg mixture, beating until well blended. Spread batter evenly into prepared pan. Bake 40 to 45 minutes or until brownies begin to pull away from sides of pan. Cool completely in pan on wire rack. Cut into bars. About 16 brownies.

VARIATION: Stir 1 cup REESE'S Peanut Butter Chips or HERSHEY'S Semi-Sweet Chocolate Chips into batter before spreading in pan.

SENSATIONAL PEPPERMINT PATTIE BROWNIES

1½ cups (3 sticks) butter or
  margarine, melted
3 cups sugar
1 tablespoon vanilla extract
5 eggs
2 cups all-purpose flour

1 cup HERSHEY'S Cocoa
1 teaspoon baking powder
1 teaspoon salt
24 small (1½-inch) YORK Peppermint
  Patties, unwrapped

Heat oven to 350°F.(325°F. for glass baking dish). Grease 13x9x2-inch baking pan. In large bowl with spoon or wire whisk, stir together butter, sugar and vanilla. Add eggs; stir until well blended. Stir in flour, cocoa, baking powder and salt; blend well. Reserve 2 cups batter; set aside. Spread remaining batter in prepared pan. Arrange peppermint patties in single layer over batter, about ½ inch apart. Spread reserved 2 cups batter over patties. Bake 50 to 55 minutes or until brownies begin to pull away from sides of pan. Cool completely in pan on wire rack; cut into squares. About 36 brownies.

TRIPLE CHOCOLATE BROWNIES

½ cup (1 stick) butter or margarine,
  softened
1 cup sugar
2 eggs
1 teaspoon vanilla extract
1¼ cups all-purpose flour
¼ cup HERSHEY'S Cocoa

¼ teaspoon baking soda
¾ cup HERSHEY'S Syrup
1 cup HERSHEY'S Semi-Sweet
  Chocolate Chips
CHOCOLATE BUTTERCREAM
  FROSTING (page 12)

Heat oven to 350°F. Grease 9-inch square baking pan. In large mixer bowl, beat butter, sugar, eggs and vanilla until light and fluffy. Stir together flour, cocoa and baking soda; add alternately with syrup to butter mixture. Stir in chocolate chips. Spread into prepared pan. Bake 40 to 45 minutes or until brownies begin to pull away from sides of pan. Cool. Frost with CHOCOLATE BUTTERCREAM FROSTING. Cut into squares. About 16 brownies.

PEANUT BUTTER AND JELLY BAR COOKIES

½ cup (1 stick) plus 2 tablespoons
  butter or margarine, softened
1¾ cups all-purpose flour, divided
½ cup plus 2 tablespoons sugar,
  divided
1 egg
½ teaspoon vanilla extract

¾ cup REESE'S Creamy or Crunchy
  Peanut Butter
½ cup plus 2 tablespoons grape jelly
  or seedless raspberry preserves
½ cup quick-cooking or regular rolled
  oats
¼ teaspoon ground cinnamon

Heat oven to 350°F. In small mixer bowl, beat ½ cup butter and ¾ cup flour until well blended. Gradually add ¾ cup flour, ½ cup sugar, egg and vanilla, blending well. Pat dough onto bottom of 9-inch square baking pan. Bake 15 minutes. Meanwhile in separate bowl, stir together peanut butter and ½ cup jelly; set aside. In small bowl, stir together oats, remaining ¼ cup flour, remaining 2 tablespoons sugar, remaining 2 tablespoons butter and cinnamon until crumbs are formed. Spread peanut butter mixture over hot crust; top with crumb mixture. Bake 20 minutes or until light brown. Cool completely in pan on wire rack. Heat remaining 2 tablespoons jelly until melted; drizzle over surface. Let stand until jelly is set. Cut into bars. About 20 bars.

BUTTERSCOTCH BLONDIES

¾ cup (1½ sticks) butter or
   margarine, softened
¾ cup packed light brown sugar
½ cup granulated sugar
2 eggs
2 cups all-purpose flour

1 teaspoon baking soda
½ teaspoon salt
1⅔ cups (10-oz. pkg.) HERSHEY'S
   Butterscotch Chips
1 cup chopped nuts (optional)

Heat oven to 350°F. Grease 13x9x2-inch baking pan. In large mixer bowl, beat butter and sugars until light and fluffy. Add eggs; blend well. In small bowl, stir together flour, baking soda and salt; gradually add to butter mixture, mixing well. Stir in butterscotch chips and nuts, if desired. Spread in prepared pan. Bake 30 to 35 minutes or until golden brown and center is set. Cool completely in pan on wire rack. Cut into bars. About 36 bars.

BUTTER PECAN SQUARES

½ cup (1 stick) butter, softened
½ cup packed light brown sugar
1 egg
1 teaspoon vanilla extract

¾ cup all-purpose flour
2 cups (11.5-oz. pkg.) HERSHEY'S
   Milk Chocolate Chips, divided
¾ cup chopped pecans, divided

Heat oven to 350°F. Grease 8-or 9-inch square baking pan. In small mixer bowl, beat butter, brown sugar, egg and vanilla until light and fluffy. Blend in flour. Stir in 1 cup milk chocolate chips and ½ cup pecans. Spread batter evenly into prepared pan. Bake 25 to 30 minutes or until lightly browned. Remove from oven. Immediately sprinkle remaining 1 cup chips over surface. Let stand 5 to 10 minutes or until chips soften; spread evenly. Immediately sprinkle remaining ¼ cup pecans over top; press gently onto chocolate. Cool completely in pan on wire rack. Cut into squares. About 16 squares.

CHOCOLATE CHIP CANDY COOKIE BARS

1⅔ cups all-purpose flour
2 tablespoons plus 1½ cups sugar,
   divided
¾ teaspoon baking powder
1 cup (2 sticks) cold butter or
   margarine, divided
1 egg, slightly beaten

2 tablespoons plus ½ cup (5-oz.can)
   evaporated milk, divided
2 cups (12-oz. pkg.) HERSHEY'S
   Semi-Sweet Chocolate Chips,
   divided
½ cup light corn syrup
1½ cups sliced almonds

Heat oven to 375°F. In medium bowl, stir together flour, 2 tablespoons sugar and baking powder; cut in ½ cup butter with pastry blender until mixture forms coarse crumbs. Stir in egg and 2 tablespoons evaporated milk; stir until mixture holds together in ball shape. Press onto bottom and ¼-inch up sides of 15½x10½x1-inch jelly roll pan. Bake 8 to 10 minutes or until lightly browned; remove from oven, leaving oven on. Sprinkle 1½ cups chocolate chips evenly over crust; do NOT disturb chips. In 3-quart saucepan, place remaining 1½ cups sugar, remaining ½ cup butter, remaining ½ cup evaporated milk and corn syrup. Cook over medium heat, stirring constantly, until mixture boils; stir in almonds. Continue cooking and stirring to 240°F on candy thermometer (soft-ball stage) or until mixture, when dropped into very cold water, forms soft ball that flattens when removed from water. Remove from heat. Immediately spoon almond mixture evenly over chips and crust; do NOT spread. Bake 10 to 15 minutes or just until almond mixture is golden brown. Remove from oven; cool 5 minutes. Sprinkle with remaining ½ cup chocolate chips; cool completely. Cut into bars. About 4 dozen bars.

PEANUT BUTTER AND CHOCOLATE CHIP PAN COOKIES

1 cup (2 sticks) butter or margarine,
   softened
¾ cup granulated sugar
¾ cup packed light brown sugar
2 eggs
½ teaspoon vanilla extract
2¼ cups all-purpose flour

1 teaspoon baking soda
½ teaspoon salt
2 cups (11.5-oz. pkg.) HERSHEY'S
   Milk Chocolate Chips
1½ cups REESE'S Peanut Butter
   Chips

Heat oven to 350°F. Grease 15½x10½x1-inch jelly-roll pan. In large mixer bowl, beat butter, granulated sugar, brown sugar, eggs and vanilla until light and fluffy. Stir together flour, baking soda and salt; add to butter mixture. Combine chocolate chips and peanut butter chips; stir into batter. Spread batter evenly into prepared pan. Bake 25 to 30 minutes or until golden brown. Cool completely in pan on wire rack. Cut into bars. About 4 dozen bars.

CHOCOLATE CHUNK BUTTER PECAN BARS

1 cup (2 sticks) butter or margarine,
   softened
1 cup packed light brown sugar
1 egg yolk

1 teaspoon vanilla extract
2 cups all-purpose flour
¼ teaspoon salt
1¾ cups (10-oz. pkg.) HERSHEY'S
   Semi-Sweet Chocolate Chunks
½ to 1 cup coarsely chopped pecans

Heat oven to 350°F. Grease 13x9x2-inch baking pan. In large mixer bowl, stir together butter, brown sugar, egg yolk and vanilla; blend in flour and salt. Press mixture onto bottom of prepared pan. Bake 25 to 30 minutes or until lightly browned. Remove from oven; immediately sprinkle chocolate chunks on crust. Let stand until softened, about 5 minutes; spread evenly over crust. Sprinkle pecans over top. Cool completely in pan on wire rack. Cut into bars. About 36 bars.

REESE'S PEANUT BUTTER BLONDIE WITH HERSHEY'S KISSES

⅓ cup butter or margarine, softened
¾ cup packed light brown sugar
½ cup REESE'S Creamy or Crunchy
   Peanut Butter
1 egg
½ teaspoon vanilla extract

¼ cup milk
1 cup all-purpose flour
¾ teaspoon baking powder
¼ teaspoon baking soda
20 HERSHEY'S KISSES Chocolates,
   unwrapped

Heat oven to 350°F. Lightly grease 9-inch square baking pan. In small mixer bowl, beat butter, brown sugar and peanut butter until well blended. Add egg and vanilla; beat well. Gradually add milk; beat until smooth. Stir together flour, baking powder and baking soda; gradually add to peanut butter mixture, beating until well blended. Spread batter in prepared pan. Bake 25 to 30 minutes or until bars begin to pull away from sides of pan and wooden pick inserted in center comes out clean. Lightly press chocolate pieces onto surface, placing in even rows of five. Cool completely in pan on wire rack. Cut into bars. About 20 bars.

FIVE LAYER BARS

¾ cup (1½ sticks) butter or margarine
1¾ cups graham cracker crumbs
¼ cup HERSHEY'S Cocoa
2 tablespoons sugar
1 can (14 oz.) sweetened condensed
    milk

1 cup (6-oz. pkg.) HERSHEY'S Semi-
    Sweet Chocolate Chips
1 cup raisins, chopped dried apricots
    or miniature marshmallows
1 cup chopped nuts

Heat oven to 350°F. Place butter in 13x9x2-inch baking pan. Heat in oven until melted; remove pan from oven. Stir together crumbs, cocoa and sugar; sprinkle evenly over butter. Pour sweetened condensed milk evenly over crumb mixture. Sprinkle with chocolate chips and raisins. Sprinkle nuts on top; press down firmly. Bake 25 to 30 minutes or until lightly browned. Cool completely in pan on wire rack. Cover with foil; let stand at room temperature 6 to 8 hours. About 36 bars.

GOLDEN BARS: Substitute 1 cup REESE'S Peanut Butter Chips for chocolate chips. Sprinkle 1 cup golden raisins or chopped dried apricots over chips. Proceed as above.

PEANUT BUTTER KISS BARS

½ cup REESE'S Creamy Peanut
    Butter
¼ cup (½ stick) butter or margarine,
    softened
1 cup packed light brown sugar
2 eggs

1 teaspoon vanilla extract
⅔ cup all-purpose flour
1 cup chopped salted peanuts, divided
16 HERSHEY'S KISSES Chocolates,
    unwrapped

Heat oven to 350°F. Grease 9-inch square baking pan. In small mixer bowl, beat peanut butter, butter and brown sugar until well blended. Add eggs and vanilla; beat until light and fluffy. Gradually add flour to butter mixture, beating until well blended. Stir in ¾ cup chopped peanuts; spread batter evenly in prepared pan. Sprinkle remaining ¼ cup peanuts over top. Bake 25 to 30 minutes or until lightly browned. Remove from oven; immediately press chocolate piece into top, allowing space for cutting into bars. Cool completely in pan on wire rack. Cut into bars. About 16 bars.

S'MORE COOKIE BARS

½ cup (1 stick) butter or margarine,
    softened
¾ cup sugar
1 egg
1 teaspoon vanilla extract
1⅓ cups all-purpose flour

¾ cup graham cracker crumbs
1 teaspoon baking powder
¼ teaspoon salt
4 HERSHEY'S Milk Chocolate Bars
    (1.55 oz. each)
1 cup marshmallow creme

Heat oven to 350°F. Grease 8-inch square baking pan. In mixer bowl, beat butter and sugar until light and fluffy. Add egg and vanilla; beat well. Stir together flour, graham cracker crumbs, baking powder and salt; add to butter mixture, beating until blended. Spread half of dough in prepared pan. Arrange chocolate bars over dough, breaking as needed to fit. Spread with marshmallow creme. Scatter bits of remaining dough over marshmallow; carefully spread to form a layer. Bake 30 to 35 minutes or until done. Cool in pan on wire rack. Cut into bars. 16 bars.

PEANUT BUTTER GLAZED CHOCOLATE BARS

¾ cup (1½ sticks) butter or margarine
½ cup HERSHEY'S Cocoa
1½ cups sugar
1½ teaspoons vanilla extract
3 eggs
1¼ cups all-purpose flour

¼ teaspoon baking powder
PEANUT BUTTER FILLING AND
   GLAZE (recipe follows)
CHOCOLATE DRIZZLE (recipe
   follows)

Heat oven to 350°F. Line 15½x10½x1-inch jelly-roll pan with foil; grease foil. In medium saucepan over low heat, melt butter. Add cocoa; stir constantly until smooth. Remove from heat; stir in sugar and vanilla. Beat in eggs, one at a time, until well combined. Stir in flour and baking powder. Spread batter evenly in prepared pan. Bake 14 to 16 minutes or until top springs back when touched lightly in center. Remove from oven; cool 2 minutes. Invert onto wire rack. Peel off foil; turn right side up on wire rack to cool completely. Prepare PEANUT BUTTER FILLING AND GLAZE. Cut brownie in half crosswise; spread half of glaze evenly on one half. Top with second half; spread with remaining glaze. Cool until glaze is set. Prepare CHOCOLATE DRIZZLE; drizzle over peanut butter glaze. After chocolate is set, cut into bars. About 40 bars.

PEANUT BUTTER FILLING AND GLAZE: In small saucepan over medium heat, stir together ¼ cup sugar and ¼ cup water; heat to boiling. Remove from heat; immediately add 1⅔ cups (10-oz. pkg.) REESE'S Peanut Butter Chips. Stir until melted. Cool slightly. About 1¼ cups glaze.

CHOCOLATE DRIZZLE: In microwave-safe bowl, place ⅓ cup HERSHEY'S Semi-Sweet Chocolate Chips and 1 teaspoon shortening. Microwave at HIGH (100%) 30 seconds to 1 minute or chips are melted and mixture is smooth when stirred.

HERSHEY BAR SQUARES

½ cup (1 stick) butter or margarine
½ cup granulated sugar
¼ cup packed light brown sugar
1 cup all-purpose flour
¾ cup quick-cooking rolled oats

¼ teaspoon baking soda
¼ teaspoon salt
1 HERSHEY'S Milk Chocolate Bar (7
   oz.), broken into pieces
1 tablespoon shortening

Heat oven to 350°F. Grease 8-inch square baking pan. In mixer bowl, beat butter, granulated sugar and brown sugar until creamy. Stir together flour, oats, baking soda and salt; gradually add to butter mixture, beating until well blended. Mixture will be crumbly. Reserve ¾ cup of crumbs for topping; press remaining crumbs onto bottom of prepared pan. Bake 15 minutes; remove from oven. Meanwhile, in top of double boiler, over hot, not boiling water, place chocolate bar pieces; stir constantly until melted. Remove from over water; spread evenly over top of baked layer. Sprinkle reserved crumbs evenly over top of chocolate; with back of spoon, gently press crumbs into chocolate. Return to oven. Bake 10 minutes or until crumbs are lightly browned. Cool completely in pan on wire rack. Cut into squares. About 25 squares.

CHOCOLATE-PEANUT BUTTER CHIP BARS

⅔ cup butter or margarine, softened
⅔ cup shortening
1 cup granulated sugar
1 cup packed light brown sugar
2 teaspoons vanilla extract
4 eggs

2¼ cups all-purpose flour
½ cup HERSHEY'S Cocoa
1 teaspoon baking powder
1 teaspoon salt
1⅔ cups (10-oz. pkg.) REESE'S
    Peanut Butter Chips

Heat oven to 350°F. Grease and flour two 9-inch square baking pans. In large mixer bowl, beat butter, shortening, granulated sugar, brown sugar and vanilla until light and fluffy. Add eggs, one at a time, beating well after each addition. In bowl, stir together flour, cocoa, baking powder and salt. Gradually add to butter mixture; beat until smooth and well blended. Stir in peanut butter chips. Spread batter in prepared pans. Bake 30 to 35 minutes or until wooden pick inserted in center comes out clean. Cool in pan on wire rack; cut into bars. About 32 bars.

PEANUT BUTTER CHIPS AND JELLY BARS

1½ cups all-purpose flour
½ cup sugar
¾ teaspoon baking powder
½ cup (1 stick) cold butter or
    margarine

1 egg, beaten
¾ cup grape jelly
1⅔ cups (10-oz. pkg.) REESE'S
    Peanut Butter Chips, divided

Heat oven to 375°F. Grease 9-inch square baking pan. Stir together flour, sugar and baking powder; with pastry blender or fork, cut in butter until mixture resembles coarse crumbs. Add egg; blend well. Reserve half of mixture; press remaining mixture onto bottom of prepared pan. Spread jelly evenly over crust. Sprinkle 1 cup peanut butter chips over jelly. Stir together remaining crumb mixture with remaining ⅔ cup chips; sprinkle over top. Bake 25 to 30 minutes or until lightly browned. Cool completely in pan on wire rack. Cut into bars. About 16 bars.

SCRUMPTIOUS CHOCOLATE LAYER BARS

2 cups (12-oz. pkg.) HERSHEY'S
    Semi-Sweet Chocolate Chips
1 package (8 oz.) cream cheese
⅔ cup (5-oz. can) evaporated milk
1 cup chopped walnuts
¼ cup sesame seeds (optional)
1 teaspoon almond extract, divided

3 cups all-purpose flour
1½ cups sugar
1 teaspoon baking powder
½ teaspoon salt
1 cup (2 sticks) butter or regular
    margarine
2 eggs

Heat oven to 375°F. Grease 13x9x2-inch baking pan. In medium saucepan, combine chocolate chips, cream cheese and evaporated milk; cook over low heat, stirring constantly, until chips are melted and mixture is blended. Remove from heat; stir in walnuts, sesame seeds, if desired, and ½ teaspoon almond extract. Blend well; set aside. Stir together remaining ingredients; blend well with electric mixer until mixture resembles coarse crumbs. Press half of crumb mixture into prepared pan; spread with chocolate mixture. Sprinkle remaining crumbs over filling. Bake 35 to 40 minutes or until golden brown. Cool completely in pan on wire rack. Cut into bars. About 36 bars.

BEVERAGES

HOT CHOCOLATE WITH PEPPERMINT

10 small (1½ inch) YORK Peppermint
Patties, unwrapped and quartered

3 cups hot milk

Place peppermint patties pieces in blender container. Add hot milk. Cover; blend until smooth. Pour into mugs. Makes 3½ cups.

PEANUT BUTTER BANANA MILKSHAKE

½ large, ripe banana, sliced
2 to 3 tablespoons REESE'S Creamy
Peanut Butter

1 cup milk
2 scoops vanilla ice cream

In blender container, place banana, peanut butter and milk. Cover; blend well. Add ice cream; cover and blend until smooth. Serve immediately. About two 8-oz. servings.

YORK PEPPERMINT COFFEE AU LAIT

1 cup (½ pt.) whipping cream, half
and half or milk
12 small (1½ inch) YORK Peppermint
Patties, unwrapped and quartered

Hot coffee
Whipped cream (optional)

In medium microwave-safe bowl, place whipping cream and peppermint pattie pieces. Microwave at HIGH (100%) 1½ minutes; pour into blender container or food processor. Cover, blend until smooth. Pour desired amount of cream mixture (¼ to ½ cup) into cups or mugs. Fill with hot coffee. Garnish with whipped cream, if desired. About 1½ cups cream mixture.

CREAMY HOT CHOCOLATE

1 can (14 oz.) sweetened condensed
milk
½ cup HERSHEY'S Cocoa

1½ teaspoons vanilla extract
⅛ teaspoon salt
6½ cups water

In large saucepan, combine sweetened condensed milk, cocoa, vanilla and salt; mix well. Gradually add water, stirring constantly. Cook over medium heat, stirring occasionally, until hot (do not boil). 8 to 10 servings.

VARIATIONS:
MARSHMALLOW CREME: Top each serving with spoonful marshmallow creme.

PEANUT BUTTER: Decrease vanilla to 1 teaspoon. Add ½ cup REESE'S Creamy Peanut Butter just before adding water.

CINNAMON CANDY: Decrease vanilla to 1 teaspoon. Add ¼ cup red cinnamon candies just before adding water.

PANCAKE SYRUP: Decrease vanilla to 1 teaspoon. Stir ½ cup pancake syrup into hot cocoa before serving.

MICROWAVE: In 2-quart glass measure, combine all ingredients. Microwave at HIGH (100%) 8 to 10 minutes, stirring every 3 minutes. Top with marshmallows, if desired.

CHOCO PEANUT BUTTER SHAKE

¾ cup cold milk
¼ cup REESE'S Creamy Peanut
   Butter

3 tablespoons HERSHEY'S Cocoa
1 tablespoon marshmallow creme
2 cups (1 pt.) vanilla ice cream

In blender container, place milk, peanut butter, cocoa and marshmallow creme. Cover; blend. Add ice cream. Cover; blend until smooth. Serve immediately. About three 6-oz. servings.

RICH AND CREAMY COCOA

3 tablespoons sugar
2 tablespoons HERSHEY'S European
   Style Cocoa
¼ cup water
1¼ cups milk

½ cup light cream
½ teaspoon vanilla extract
PEPPERMINT CREAM TOPPING or
   MOCHA CREAM TOPPING
   (optional, recipes follow)

In medium saucepan, combine sugar and cocoa; add water, stirring well. Cook over medium heat, stirring constantly, until mixture boils. Stir in milk and light cream. Heat to serving temperature. Do not boil. Remove from heat; add vanilla. Serve immediately. Garnish with desired topping. About 3 servings.

PEPPERMINT CREAM TOPPING: In small mixer bowl, combine ½ cup cold whipping cream, 2 tablespoons sugar, 1 tablespoon HERSHEY'S European Style Cocoa, ½ teaspoon vanilla extract and ⅛ teaspoon peppermint extract; beat until stiff.

MOCHA CREAM TOPPING: In small mixer bowl, combine ½ cup cold whipping cream, 2 tablespoons sugar, 1 tablespoon HERSHEY'S European Style Cocoa, 1 teaspoon powdered instant coffee and ½ teaspoon vanilla extract; beat until stiff.

FLAVORED HOT COCOA MIX

4 cups nonfat dry milk powder
1½ cups sugar
1 cup HERSHEY'S Cocoa

1 cup powdered non-dairy creamer
Flavoring (suggestions follow)

In large bowl, stir together all ingredients with wire whisk. Add one of the flavors suggested below; with wire whisk, stir until well blended. Store mix in tightly sealed jar.

To prepare single serving: place ¼ cup mix in cup or mug. Stir in ¾ cup boiling water; mix well. About 7½ cups mix (about thirty 6-oz. servings).

FLAVOR VARIATIONS:
COCONUT: Add 2 tablespoons coconut extract and 2 teaspoons vanilla extract.

ORANGE: Add 2 tablespoons orange extract.

MINT: Add 2 teaspoons mint extract and 2 teaspoons vanilla extract.

MOCHA: Add ¼ cup powdered instant coffee.

INDEX OF RECIPES

HERSHEY'S
Coupons

Save 25¢

| MANUFACTURER COUPON | EXPIRES 12/31/97 |

25¢

on any **HERSHEY'S Baking Chocolate**

00269

25¢

5 34000 32125 9

Save 25¢

| MANUFACTURER COUPON | EXPIRES 12/31/97 |

25¢

on any **HERSHEY'S Cocoa**

00270

25¢

5 34000 32025 2

Save 50¢

| MANUFACTURER COUPON | EXPIRES 12/31/97 |

50¢

on any size or style of **REESE'S™ Peanut Butter**

00216

50¢

5 34000 38050 8

Save 25¢

25¢

on any HERSHEY'S/REESE'S Chips

00271

25¢

RETAILER: We will redeem coupon for face value plus 8¢ handling if submitted in compliance with Hershey's redemption policy, incorporated herein by reference. Void if reproduced or where prohibited by law. Good only in the U.S.A. Cash value 1/20¢. Mail to: Hershey Foods Corporation, CMS Department #34000, One Fawcett Drive, Del Rio, TX 78840. LIMIT ONE COUPON PER PURCHASE.

5 34000 31025 3

Save 25¢

25¢

on any flavor of HERSHEY'S Chocolate Shoppe Topping

00274

25¢

RETAILER: We will redeem coupon for face value plus 8¢ handling if submitted in compliance with Hershey's redemption policy, incorporated herein by reference. Void if reproduced or where prohibited by law. Good only in the U.S.A. Cash value 1/20¢. Mail to: Hershey Foods Corporation, CMS Department #34000, One Fawcett Drive, Del Rio, TX 78840. LIMIT ONE COUPON PER PURCHASE.

5 34000 33825 7

HERSHEY'S
Makes it Chocolate!

Save 30¢

30¢

on any 6 oz. bag (or larger) of YORK Miniatures

00229

30¢

RETAILER: We will redeem coupon for face value plus 8¢ handling if submitted in compliance with Hershey's redemption policy, incorporated herein by reference. Void if reproduced or where prohibited by law. Good only in the U.S.A. Cash value 1/20¢. Mail to: Hershey Foods Corporation, CMS Department #34000, One Fawcett Drive, Del Rio, TX 78840. LIMIT ONE COUPON PER PURCHASE.

5 34000 22530 4

Save 25¢

25¢

on any **HERSHEY'S Giant Bar** (6 oz. or larger)

00264

25¢

5 34000 14525 1

Save 25¢

25¢

on one 6-pack of
HERSHEY'S Milk
Chocolate or **Milk Chocolate with Almonds**

00262

25¢

5 34000 12125 5

Save 25¢

25¢

on any size
HERSHEY'S
Special Dark

00263

25¢

5 34000 10025 0